Heitons—A Managed Transition

Other books by Tony Farmar

A History of Craig Gardner—the first hundred years (1988)

The Legendary Lofty Clattery Café—Bewleys of Ireland (1988)

Ordinary Lives—the private lives of three generations of Ireland's professional classes (1991)

Holles Street 1894–1994 (1994)

A Brief History of Clé: The Irish Book Publishers' Association (1995)

With Peter Costello

The Very Heart of the City—the story of Denis Guiney and Clerys (1992)

Heitons—A Managed Transition

*Heitons in the Irish coal,
iron and building markets,
1818–1996*

Tony Farmar

A. & A. Farmar
1996

British Library Cataloguing in Publication
Data
A CIP catalogue record for this book is
available from the British Library

Cover design by Source
Copy-editing by Pat Carroll
Index by Helen Litton
Design and typesetting by A. & A. Farmar
Printed by Betaprint

ISBN 0 899047 21 2

A. & A. Farmar
Beech House
78 Ranelagh Village
Dublin 6
Ireland

Contents

Acknowledgements   VI

Chairman's Foreword   VII

1. The Black Black Coal 1818–1850s   I

2. Brought from Across the Water 1850–1896   14

3. The First Years of the Public
    Company 1896–1910   32

4. The Glare of Public Limelight 1910–1920   50

5. Wars and Rumours of Wars 1920–1939   70

6. In Plato's Cave 1939–1957   91

7. All is Changed 1958–1974   108

8. A Managed Transition 1975–1996   124

    Appendixes

1. Directors and Principal Officers   146

2. Heitons' Fleet   149

3. The Hewat Family in Heitons   153

    Endnotes   154

    Index   160

Acknowledgements

THE PRINCIPAL DEBT INCURRED during the writing of this book has been to Sid Kane, who joined the firm in 1946 and retired in 1988 after twenty-four years as Company Secretary. He led me through the mysteries of coal and shipping, and was a constant source of information about the company and its customs. The book is largely based on the Heiton archives, of which his knowledge is unrivalled. Without his guidance and help the book would certainly have been very much the poorer. The appendixes, on the directors and principal officers, the firm's fleet and the Hewat family, were researched and compiled by him.

Sid himself wishes to thank for their help in the research, Joe Henry, Superintendent, Mercantile Marine Office, Department of the Marine; Philip Booth, the Maritime Institute of Ireland (and co-incidentally a great-grandson of William Hewat I); Della Murphy and Gregory O'Connor of the National Archives, and the staff of the Gilbert Library in Pearse Street.

I am grateful too for information and ready assistance in the course of writing from Catherine Condell and her sister Ann Murray, and from Leo Martin and Charlie Craig. Particular thanks are due to Richard Hewat for initiating and, pleasantly but persistently, driving forward what I found a fascinating piece of Irish business and social history.

The photographs are from the company archive, except four which are by kind permission of the late Cliff Eager's family.

Chairman's Foreword

LIKE ANY ORGANISATION THAT has been around for more than a hundred years, Heitons has changed greatly over time. As this history records, it began as quite a small coal and iron importing business, and for a hundred and fifty years industrial and domestic coal were its mainstays. When coal was even more important to factories, offices and homes than oil and gas are now, the Heitons' name was synonymous with high quality coal, shipped into Dublin on its own handsome vessels. There was also a steady sale for the metal and hardware products of what was called the Iron Department.

Just before the Second World War the imports of coal into Ireland reached a peak. From then on coal sales began a long withdrawal. Heitons was faced, like a saddler or blacksmith of the 1920s, with a steadily declining market. There were two choices: to develop in a new and different direction, or to hang on, in the hopes that something would turn up. Heitons took the former course— the firms that took the latter option are now gone.

The housing boom of the late 1940s and the 1950s gave the small Iron Department, which up to then employed a mere thirteen people out of a total of several hundred, a chance to show its potential. The ugly duckling was about to become a swan.

As we celebrate the centenary of Heitons' incorporation in 1896, we also celebrate the management leadership and the staff dedication that enabled the firm to make that rarest and most difficult of all business transitions, from being a market leader in one highly competitive type of product to becoming a market leader in quite another. For Heitons is now the largest builders' merchants and steel stockholder in the country and a market leader in the homecare/DIY business.

Reading Tony Farmar's history, it seemed to me that a number of factors accounted for Heitons' achievement. These were:

- constantly providing the best quality the market demanded;
- continuous investment in process improvement and innovation;
- very precise cost accounting, to the extent that every lorry and crane had to pay its way;
- very strong staff loyalty—service with the company of forty or fifty years was common;
- very close attention by the directors to operational details;
- consciousness that activities presently contributing relatively small profits may be the source of organic growth in the long term.

As a recipe for corporate success, it is difficult to see what is missing, apart perhaps from the element of luck, which is at no-one's bidding.

I hope that this *History* will help the firm to sustain its present successes, by inculcating these lessons, and perhaps also the subtler lesson that even in the hurly-burly of immediate business pressure, the short-term view is not the only one to consider.

Stephen O'Connor
Chairman

Chapter 1
The Black Black Coal
1818–1850s

THE FIRST TASK EVERY MORNING, in homes and workshops throughout Dublin, was to light the fire. At the earliest hour sleepy tweenies and stout boilermen rekindled life into the kitchen range, the breakfast-room fire and the boiler house. Coal heated the tea and chased the chill off the day in frowsty city centre tenement rooms housing families of six or more, and in spacious Shrewsbury Road houses with an acre of garden and five rooms to each person. Coal also drove the steam engines that provided power to all kinds of operations from lathes to printing machines. It was coal that lit Guinness's boilers, that fired Jamesons and Jacobs, that urged forward the great railway engines pulling goods and passengers from Broadstone and Amiens Street to the far corners of the country. It was coal that provided most of the warmth and power that made the city habitable.

Although there were mines in Ireland, they never provided anything like enough to meet the needs of a growing economy. Consequently most coal came from Britain. Like a steady infusion of warming black blood, coal was dragged in great wagons from mines in Wales and the Black Country to quays in Liverpool or Cardiff, then poured into grimy, blunt-nosed, unglamorous colliers which butted and crashed their way across the Irish Sea in all weathers. At the quayside in Dublin it was laboriously hauled out of the holds, put into more wagons, or carefully weighed out into sacks (sixteen to the ton) for the draymen. These hardy souls, working through the winter with often no more than an empty sack across their shoulders for a coat, each had their beat, their connection of households. Fanning out across the city, this one to Ranelagh, that to Drumcondra, the draymen and their patient horses laden with a ton or so at a batch called to street after street. A middle-class household would use about a ton a month—more if a nursery fire was kept lit all day. Usually the coal was delivered down a specially prepared chute, straight into the coal hole. Sack after sack of coal was humped manually off the dray, across the front garden, and poured with a slithering crash down the chute. The next morning Bridie would fill her coal scuttle, and perhaps no more than weeks since it was hacked from the deep earth, the inherited warmth of the Carboniferous era would be set to boiling a kettle.

For most of its history the firm of Thomas Heiton was best known to the public for coal. Every year the firm shipped into Ireland tens of thousands of tons of coal for household and industrial use. It was one of the leading coal importing and merchanting houses, deploying a small army of dockers, bagmen, draymen and others to ensure the vital supply. One of Heitons' proudest tales describes how in 1926, during the British General Strike, over 100,000 tons of coal were imported from America, at a loss, to ensure that the city's industries and hospitals were kept alive.

Unlike other coal merchants, however, Heitons always had another side to the business—the Iron Department, as it was called. This had been started at the beginning of the nineteenth century with the importation of 'bar iron' to meet the needs of blacksmiths and wheelwrights. Over time it expanded into machine tools and hardware, with a fabricating shop (a sort of modern urban version of the smithy) where special metalworking requirements could be met. The firm prided itself on being able to supply anything from a needle to an anchor. The coal and iron sides of the business ran side by side, separately staffed and each expected to make its own profit.

This also applied to the Shipping Department, which ran the boats that brought the goods from abroad.

Although the Iron Department was for many years very much the lesser partner in the business, it was the origin of the present configuration. Heiton Holdings' steel, builders' merchants and homecare/DIY divisions spring directly from the old Iron Department. For the coal business was not to last (at least not more than 150 years!). Cleaner, less cumbersome fuels were to replace coal. The establishment of the Shannon hydroelectric scheme in 1925, with the capacity to meet more than two and a half times the nation's electrical needs, was the first straw in the wind. Imports of coal into the Republic reached a peak in 1938 with some 2.5 million tonnes, sinking to 1 million by 1967. To those with eyes to see, the writing was on the wall. In 1946, with uncanny precision, the author of the previous history of the firm, Company Secretary J. Denham Macalister, wrote: 'perhaps when the time to celebrate our centenary comes, the coal trade as we know it may be a thing of the past. Perhaps we will have completed the circle and gone back to building.'[1] In 1995 (a year before the centenary of the firm's incorporation in 1896) Heitons finally sold its last interest in coal, and became a business based on builders' merchanting, steel and homecare/DIY.

The firm's name entered the Dublin business world in 1818 when young Thomas Heiton came to Dublin from Scotland and was apprenticed to Thomas Ashley's new coal and iron business which was based in City Quay. Thomas Ashley was born about 1780, and had worked with his father, who was a prominent timber and slate merchant, and also ran a small building business. In 1817 he married Isabella Heiton from Melrose, a small town on the Tweed in Scotland. Isabella had come over to Dublin a few years before to look after her uncle, James Heiton, who had been connected with the building trade in Beresford Place since 1795.

Thomas Heiton was born in Melrose, Scotland in 1804. In 1818 he followed his sister to Dublin to work in his brother–in–law's business in City Quay. The family lived in Roundtown (as Terenure was then called). In 1833 Thomas married Jane Francis Quigly, and the newly–weds moved into a little house sentimentally called Melrose Villa on Rathgar Road. By the time Thomas Ashley died in 1868, Heiton had been carrying on a business as coal and iron factor in his own name for thirty–five years. However, since the business was carried on from the same premises as those of Thomas Ashley, it seems that they maintained close connections. As we shall see in the next chapter, many of the import activities were done on a cargo–at–a–time basis, which facilitated a series of loose relationships between various factors. Another person involved in these 'adventures' was Gilbert Burns, who was also a partner of William Todd, with whom he ran the drapery and department store Todd, Burns of Mary Street.

In 1818 Ireland and the world were digesting the effects of the ending of the Revolutionary and Napoleonic wars between France and Britain that had lasted for virtually twenty years. The long peace of the nineteenth century started in 1815 when Napoleon was at last despatched to the fastness of St Helena. In November 1818, as Thomas Heiton was settling in to his new life, the victorious countries, Austria, Great Britain, Prussia and Russia finally withdrew their troops from France and the King, Louis XVIII, set up his own ministry. The first steam vessel crossed the Atlantic in 1818, taking 26 days to do it. In the United States of America, Illinois had just been admitted to the Union, and treaties were being negotiated with the Chicksaws, the Great and Little Osages, the Quapaw and the Choctaw. Thirty years later this last tribe was to endear itself to the Irish people by its generous donations during the Famine.

Ireland was even then staggering under its problems. In a society where many habitually lived close to starvation, between 1816 and 1818 a series of poor harvests and epidemics had caused great hardship. The weather was continuously cold and wet, inhibiting the growing of potatoes and preventing turf from being dried sufficiently. Depressed by cold and hunger, the people were ready victims to out-breaks of smallpox and typhus. These diseases, often brought in from the country by itinerant workers, thrived in the appalling conditions of the Dublin tenements. The fever hospitals were swamped, and new ones were (eventually) founded. During these three years, in this grim rehearsal for the greater famine thirty years later, possibly 100,000 people died out of a population of some 7 million.

Soldiers returning from the war found a still backward country—it was relatively little urbanised, and two–fifths of the population lived in more or less wretched one–roomed cabins or tenements. While life was miserable at the bottom of the heap, for the 10,000 landlords and the 150,000 or so strong farmers, it was as comfortable as the early nineteenth century allowed. In the cities the professions flourished, and the lawyers and the medical men moved their families into the great urban houses vacated after the Act of Union, and set about recre-ating society in their own image.

The young Thomas Heiton would no doubt have been struck on arrival by the splendour of Dublin, which really was the second city of the Empire. Visitors were greatly impressed by its 'noble avenues and the splendour of the houses.'[2] Sir Walter Scott described the city as 'splendid beyond my expectations'. 'The traveller to Dublin finds the approach as imposing as when he visited London,' wrote Frederick Engels. 'Dublin Bay is the most impressive in the British Isles . . . the city itself is most attractive and its aristocratic quarter is laid out in a more tasteful manner than that of any other British town. By con-trast the poorer districts of Dublin are among the ugliest and most revolting in the world.'[3] The city was quite small, only 200,000 people, virtually all of whom lived between the canals. An increas-ing number lived in little villages outside the city, such as Blackrock, which Sir Walter Scott described as 'thick with villas and all the signs of ease and opulence'. Terenure, where the Ashleys lived, was one such village, a journey to it from Dublin costing 3s 1d by coach.

Although coal had been occasionally imported into Ireland in the

Middle Ages, typically as ballast, it wasn't until the disturbances of the late sixteenth and early seventeenth centuries that it became vital to Dublin in particular. Since the native Irish prevented the loyal inhabitants of Dublin from getting the wood they normally used for cooking and heat, the authorities encouraged them to use coal. In 1599 the Earl of Essex wrote to the Privy Council in London complaining about a new tax on coal, explaining its disastrous effects in Dublin:

> The masters of barques, finding themselves unable to answer the trade of coals at any reasonable rate, have forborne to bring up any. Dublin and other towns on the sea coast . . . are by the present rebellion debarred from the benefits of the woods in Leinster and Ulster from which they are accustomed to be well served. There will be hard living either in Dublin or in those towns on the coast.[4]

By the end of the seventeenth century Sir William Petty confirmed that coal was 'the general and uniform fuel' for the people of Dublin. He estimated that Ireland was then importing some 40,000 tons of coal every year.[5]

The profound importance of coal to the inhabitants of Dublin in particular led to the authorities passing Act after Act in an attempt to ensure an even supply and an equitable market. Long before there was anything approaching a Poor Law in Ireland, in 1761 an Act established emergency public coal yards, declaring that 'as often as the price of coals in the city of Dublin shall exceed the rate of eighteen shillings the ton, the public coal yards shall be kept open from the hour of ten in the morning to ten in the afternoon (Sunday and Christmas Day excepted)'.

Most of the coal imported into Ireland came from Cumberland. The best was from Whitehaven (near present–day Sellafield), though Workington, Harrington and Maryport in Cumberland were regular sources. Other places on the west coast, from Troon in Scotland to Swansea in Wales, also supplied coal to Ireland. The best quality was, however, from Whitehaven, which fetched a premium of 15 per cent or more on the less popular Harrington coal. The Whitehaven colliery had begun shipping coal seriously into Dublin in the middle of the seventeenth century. With adroit use of natural advantages and administrative ability, the Lowther family (later the Earls of Lonsdale), which owned the Whitehaven mines, had by 1675 driven its rivals out of the market: 'for at least a century, the Lowther family was able to maintain something closely approaching a monopoly over the sale of coal in Dublin'.[6] Of course they were occasionally tempted to exploit their dominant position. In 1729 Dean Swift urged the development of local collieries, complaining that 'when the city was starving all the winter for want of coals . . . the Whitehaven colliers imposed upon us at what prices they pleased'.[7]

When the coal ships came into the river they tied up on the quays and commenced selling coal straight from the hold. The price and quality of the coal was supposed to be shown on a notice attached to the mast. In this way the shipmasters would expect to get rid of about 50 tons a day, and be in port some five days. Any delay made the masters anxious to sell their coal and get back to sea; they were therefore vulnerable to jobbing and price haggling by the coal factors. To counter this pressure the masters would agree among each other in advance as to the prices of coal—at one point legislation tried to prevent this by forbidding prices to be fixed east of Ringsend.

Very little coal was sold at this time from yards. Coal factors such as Thomas Ashley and Thomas Heiton would buy coal at the mast–price, less a standard wholesale discount. Porters or draymen then carried the coal around the city. Ordinary citizens might also buy direct, thus hoping to cut out the middlemen. This, however, exposed them to the activities of the 'corner–boys'. Before it became a general term of abuse, this phrase referred to rogues whose special skill was to lure unsuspecting buyers on to boats carrying inferior coal, and, pretending to act as honest brokers, to arrange a sale of this coal as if it were premium quality. The shipmasters would (illegally) pay bribes to the corner–boys and the coal factors to encourage them to buy their coal.

One can readily imagine the lavish pantomime of bargaining and per-suading that the corner–boy and the master would get up for the ben-efit of their victim. The price difference was split with the master, and the corner–boy frequently got a tip from his unsuspecting victim into the bargain.[8]

Once the deal was struck, whether with the factor or anyone else, the master would summon a gang of men into the hold. Their job was to shovel the coal into a standard–sized basket and haul it up on to the quayside to be bagged for the waiting drays. One old coasting skipper remembered such a system operating in the 1920s: 'coal was discharged by shovelling into tubs and as the colliers came alongside the river berths the shore gang would come running with their shov-els asking "Which side did you load skipper?" On being told they immediately threw their shovels on that side to claim it, as they knew that the large lumps of coal shot across the ship when loading whilst the smaller coal dropped straight down and was easier to shovel!'[9]

Throughout the eighteenth century a constant stream of legisla-tion attempted to control the price and market for coal. In the early part of the century (1733) an Act forbade 'bodies politic or corpo-rate' from buying more than a certain amount of coal at once. The number of coal factors was limited to forty, and they were not al-lowed to buy or sell coal on their own account. Even their personal consumption was limited to twenty tons a year (an interestingly low indication of ordinary usage). The Lord Mayor and magistrates had the power to enter and search cellars and yards and direct that excess coals therein be sold.[10] As supply to the market became more regu-lar, this draconian Act was repealed, in 1782.

Another approach to control was to regulate in great detail the exact conditions of the point of sale. Coal was measured by bulk rather than weight, so the exact size of the measures was laid down in 1728: 'every half barrel shall be twenty five inches diameter in the bottom, and twenty five inches and a half in the top at least, and contain twenty gallons Winchester measure'.[11] The coal was to be raised by 'a winch or windlass to be fixed to the deck'. Of course, even if the proper measure were used, it was possible for those shovelling the coal in the hold to give short measure by filling the barrel quite loosely. To prevent this abuse, the 1791 Act prescribed that while the coal is being lifted out of the hold it is to be banged 'once or oftener against the combings or the side of the hatchway of such ship while such measuring–vessel shall be raising from the hold'. Any 'deficiency of measure' was to be made good immediately.

In case the shipmaster might be tempted to deter inquisitive visitors by inadequate gangplanks, the Lord Mayor was empowered to 'compel the captains, owners or keepers of such vessels to put on planks such handrails, man–rope or such other defence as he shall judge sufficient'. Finally shipmasters were not to bribe porters and others to buy their coal: 'any porter or carman or other who shall demand or receive a douceur or premium, commonly called the old man, shall for every such offence forfeit not exceeding ten pounds'.

Not all of this careful legislation was motivated by concern for the public good. Until 1831 coal was taxed, and government as usual was anxious to protect its sources of revenue. In a country largely denuded of its wood, and in the absence of good turf–drying facilities, coal was of strategic importance all along Ireland's east coast. To deprive a family of fuel was tantamount to forcing it into theft. As one early nineteenth–century lawyer with special knowledge of the coal trade wrote in the 1820s, when the memory of the Famine time of 1816–19 was still fresh:

> scarcity of fuel is alike inconsistent with the honesty of a people and the improvement of a country . . . scarcity of fuel is not more injurious to the morals than the health of this nation, and not only contributes to make property precarious and public morals insecure, but also to assist the periodic returns of those destroying epidemics by which this country is visited.[12]

What was the coal that Thomas Heiton and his colleagues imported into Ireland used for? By the middle of the nineteenth century about

40 per cent of Britain's coal was used for industrial purposes and about half for space heating, lighting or cooking—the rest was exported. In Ireland very much less would have been used industrially. The iron industry, which used one–third of British consumption, was virtually nonexistent, and many of the other industries continued to use water–power. The textile industry was dominated by water–power, and spade mills (which produced agricultural implements), breweries, distilleries and paper–mills all used water. As late as 1870 a quarter of the power used in Irish industry was generated from water. As a consequence, Dublin industry clustered along the banks of the Liffey and Dodder rivers. Robert Kane, writing in 1844, believed that turf was a potential substitute for coal, because although it delivered half the calorific value, it cost one–third the price, so was relatively cheap per calorie. The drop in coal costs after 1850 and the rise in the cost of Irish labour to save turf switched the basis of this calculation until turf ceased to have so clear an advantage. As a result, imports of coal into Ireland increased steadily during the nineteenth century, from an aver-

Table 1.1: *Coal Imported into Ireland (Selected Dates)*

Port	1818 %	1824 %	1846 %	1847 %
Dublin	46	32	33	36
Belfast	13	14	19	21
Cork	13	18	13	11
Waterford	8	8	10	8
Other ports	20	28	25	24
Total (000 tons)	573	727	1,264	964

Note: As coal usage becomes more widespread, the proportion imported through Dublin goes down. Industrial development drives Belfast's proportion up. Between 1846 and 1847 coal imported into Cork and Waterford dropped by 35 per cent, or 100,000 tons.
Sources: 1818: *Account of Coals Imported into Ireland 1818*
1824: *Select Committee on the Coal Trade* (1830)
1846/7: *Account of Tons of Sea Coal Imported into Ireland* (1849)

age of 360,000 tons a year at the time of the Act of Union (1801) to 800,000 tons by the time of the passing of the Catholic Emancipation Act (1829). By the time of the Fenian rising, forty years later, Ireland was importing 2.5 million tons a year.

Most of the coal imported into Ireland was thus for domestic use. Usage was increased gradually over the century by an important trend in Irish (indeed European) domestic history. For hundreds of years most people had lived in the country, in houses that basically consisted of a large single room—the hall—used for all domestic purposes from frolicking to cooking, with small rooms off for the elderly to sleep. A fire at one end, in a large canopied space set straight on the floor, was kept permanently 'in'. Turf or wood was constantly available to feed this centre point of the household.

Houses for the rapidly growing urban population, on the other hand, tended to consist of a number of smaller rooms, each dedicated to a particular purpose: eating, cooking, sleeping, even washing. The room directly accessible from the front door, the hall, which had been the centre of life, shrank to a mere corridor off which stairways and specialist rooms radiated. The hall became the arena for the exits and entrances of outsiders into the family's private world. It was no longer heated. The specialist rooms were heated, but only for the time they were being used. Lower–status members of the household were lucky to have a fire in their private bedroom (thus in Jane Austen's *Mansfield Park* the despised Fanny lived many years without a fire). It was some years through the century before a servant in a small household could expect to sleep anywhere but the kitchen. For the urban poor in Dublin, squatting in tenements in the houses abandoned by the upper classes, coal was an expensive necessity: the records of the Sick and Indigent Room Keepers' Society are full of reports of quantities of coal being distributed.

To get the most out of coal the fireplace required a number of special amendments, in particular a narrow chimney throat and an angling of the walls to throw as much heat as possible into the room.

The more precisely the configuration was designed for coal, the less satisfactory it was for the expansive needs of turf or wood. Until the middle of the century cooking in the kitchen was usually done on an open fire, with a variety of metal hooks and stands for utensils. By the middle of the century ranges (open or closed) were readily available.

How much coal was used obviously depended on the individual household. A Dublin official at the beginning of the nineteenth century spent £31 a year on coal and candles. We might guess he used some 3lbs of candles a week at a shilling a pound—this leaves £23 for coal, which seems a lot since he was also buying rush lights and turf.[13] He was clearly doing himself well for the time—warmth and comfort in the modern sense were not usually high priorities in the grander homes. The great stately houses of the Anglo–Irish were famously cold: 'Clothes for the old, exercise for the young and fires for cooking only' was a favourite maxim. The enormous Georgian houses were often heated on as little as twenty–four tons of coal and three trees a year.[14] For smaller households, much less would be used: in London in 1855 Mrs Carlyle reported burning about a ton a month for a household that consisted of just herself and her husband and a single servant in their Chelsea home.[15]

By the end of the century the bourgeois values of comfort and cosiness (as celebrated most famously by Dickens) had become more important. People began to expect at least some rooms in the house to be warm. In *How to Keep House* (1902), Mrs Peel writes:

> In a house with rooms of moderate size burning two sitting–room and two nursery fires (7 o' clock to 10 o' clock, for example) and two bedroom fires from 4 o' clock, the consumption of coal for the year would be about twenty tons, this allowing for the six warmer months, the kitchen fire, and two sitting–rooms and one nursery whenever required.

Few records survive of Thomas Heiton's activities in the first half of the nineteenth century. We do know, however, that as well as coal, he imported iron into Ireland. Most of this was in bar form for smithies and the wheelwrights' shops. Bar iron for horseshoes was a constant low–level requirement throughout the century when the population of horses fluctuated between 500,00 and 600,000. The second major use of bar–iron was for 'tyres' and other metal work for farm wagons and carts. For centuries the standard type of cart used in Ireland was not the heavy wagon used in rural England, (such as Constable's 'Hay Wain'), but a much lighter, simpler, vehicle with solid wheels rigidly attached to a rotating axle.

At the end of the eighteenth century, encouraged by better roads, improving landlords were importing 'Scotch carts' with spoked wheels. These wheels were made of five or six segments of wood gripped together by a rigid hoop of iron around the whole wheel—this was called a tyre. These hoops were shaped and then heated in a furnace so that they expanded just enough to be forced over the wheel. As the iron manacle cooled, the tyre shrank and gripped the segments of the wheel into a whole. The metal used in the smithies and wheelwrights' shops was imported in long iron bars, from which portions would be chiselled as necessary. The standard bars were sixteen feet long. To enable a cart to work on rough ground the axle needed to be at least two feet from the ground. By π we know that, to make a hoop to fit round a four-foot high wheel, the iron needs to be at least 12 feet long.[16]

These, then, were the market and the products that young Thomas Heiton was inducted into by his brother-in-law, and they were to be the basis of the firm's fortunes for the foreseeable future. Crucial to the business, however, was the transport system, in particular the ships used to bring coal and iron into Ireland. The early years of this system are covered in the next chapter.

Chapter 2
Brought from Across the Water
1850–1896

I T IS SAID THAT THE FIRST secret of commercial success is to be in the right business. If this is so, Thomas Ashley's move into the importation of coal and iron was extremely well timed, for coal and iron were the defining products of the nineteenth-century economy. We have seen that the use of coal in Dublin and the east coast of Ireland began in earnest in the seventeenth century. At the beginning of that century a mere 3,000 tons a year were being imported; by 1700, the citizens of Dublin (who took at least two-thirds of the national importation) used 40,000 tons a year.[1] The rise continued: 'in 1783 the quantity was 230,000 tons,' wrote Henry O'Hara in 1866, 'and in 1804 it amounted to 417,000 tons. These importations have increased amazingly, not only for consumption in the seaport town, but to meet the requirements of inland districts.'[2]

The demand for coal began to grow exponentially when it was combined with iron in the steam engine, which in turn powered the numerous machines of the Victorian factory. Coal became to the Victorian age what oil is to us. It provided power, light and heat; it meant industrial development, power and wealth; its exploitation was a symbol of humanity's increasing dominance over Nature. It was central to domestic comfort as well as to business growth.

When connected with the steam engine, it was the miracle mover of the age—one author notes that:

by 1800 the United Kingdom [including Ireland] was using perhaps 11 million tons of coal a year; by 1830 the amount had doubled; fifteen years later it had doubled again; and by 1870 it was crossing the 100-million ton mark. This last was the equivalent to 800 million calories of energy, enough to feed a population of 850 million adults a year.[3]

Suddenly the industrialist was presented with a source of power that didn't get tired, or sick, or go on strike. With this opportunity, and an ever-widening commercial empire in which to sell the goods, British industrialists created the mass production factory.

Conservatives and socialists were simultaneously excited and concerned about the social potential of the new system. The reaction of Elizabeth Smith, a landlord's wife from Baltiboys in County Wicklow, was typical. Visiting the Irish Exhibition of 1853 (in the grounds of Leinster House), she saw a model factory in one of the halls.

Models of every one of these beautiful helps to labour, these creators of wealth, and alas! to say, these corrupters of our purer nature, are here at full work. From the chopping asunder of iron bars, to the ribbon loom weaving, and the pottery wheel, we have a sample of each steam-driven manufacture throughout our toiling country. Interesting beyond idea, melancholy to reflect on, for what does this over labour do? Enriches the few, enslaves the many, loosens principles . . . factory life, a life of sin, unnatural, deleterious, revolting. Through all the grandeur of these wonderful machines, wonderful in their construction, wonderful in their produce, wonderful from the long chain of human skill and human toil attending the dispersion of their wonderful creations, I see in my sad mind's eye, the workman's home—cold bare dirty unregulated; low sensuality its pleasure, discontent the spirit pervading it.[4]

For various reasons, industrialisation never reached the same intensity in Ireland as in Britain, indeed there is evidence that the degree of industrialisation achieved by 1821 actually declined over the following years. The 1853 Exhibition cashed in on the vogue for exhibitions, but as one historian put it, 'offered a gloomy assessment of Irish manufacturing . . . most Irish exhibitors were strictly small-time producers, or else importers of English wares'.[5]

When coal began to come to Dublin regularly in the seventeenth century, it was in tiny cargoes of less than 50 tons; one reason the Whitehaven colliery maintained its dominance over the Dublin market in the early eighteenth century was its investment in 'monster' colliers capable of importing 150–200 tons at a time.[6] By the early nineteenth century a regular trade was established across the Irish Sea, in sailing colliers carrying lots of 200 or 250 tons. Although Whitehaven coal was still the dominant brand, and the consumers' favourite, and most of the rest came from other ports along Britain's west coast such as Liverpool, Milford, Cardiff and Bristol, a few vessels came from as far away as Newcastle and Exeter.

To reduce the need for the cumbersome and expensive transport of coal by land, these small boats called in to a great number of separate ports on the coast. The 1818 *Account of Coals Imported into Ireland* lists twenty-six ports into which coal was delivered in 1818.[7] (A hundred years later a report to Dáil Eireann noted that there were as many as 73 harbours importing coal.) Most of the ports taking coal in 1818 were to the east of the line from Coleraine to Cork. The west coast took much less: imports to Galway, Limerick and Sligo together accounted for less than 4 per cent of the whole. The *Account* reports the importation in 1818 of 632,376˘ tons (the precision of the ˘ somehow fails to inspire confidence). The biggest port was Dublin, taking 42 per cent, and the next biggest were Belfast and Cork with 12 per cent each. Such was the enormous increase in the demand for coal that as early as 1846 twice as much, or nearly 1.3 million tons, was being imported into Ireland, and Belfast was now taking as much as 19 per cent.

Although steam ships were plying the seas, notably as passenger ferries, they were still expensive, and the paddle steamer arrangement, which required a central engine, did not allow the kind of large deep hold that coal required. The ships used for importing coal were usually two-masted brigs or brigantines, with a sail plan not far removed from that familiar to Drake and the other Elizabethan heroes. The two-mast rig allowed plenty of room for a spacious cargo hold, was more manoeuvrable, and also used far fewer crew than the three-masted square rig used by the ocean-going merchant or fighting ships. On the other hand, the amount of sail it was possible to carry on two masts limited the carrying capacity of the colliers.

The first vessel owned by Thomas Heiton was the brig *Albion*, which had been built in 1838 and acquired around 1845. The *Syren*, built in 1845 especially for Heitons, was also a brig. The third boat known to have been acquired by Heitons, the *North Ash*, built in 1810 and acquired in 1860, was a schooner. This rig had fore-and-aft sails on both main and foremast, thus reducing the number of men required to go aloft to tend to the sails, and so was particularly economic on crew. Schooners exchanged power for a smaller crew and greater ability to manoeuvre against contrary winds. A fore-and-aft rigged schooner could sail at four points off the wind (45 degrees) while a square rigged vessel could achieve only six points (67.5 degrees). This would have been a great advantage in crossing the Irish Sea constantly facing into the prevailing wind.

Conditions on these sailing colliers were rough, and national and international regulation was slight. Ships did not carry sidelights, no international rule of the road at sea existed; there were no international code signals; neither reports of wrecks nor inquiries as to the cause of wrecks had been instituted; the famous Plimsoll line, designed to prevent overloading of ships, was not to come until the end of the century; and there was no statutory control over the food or accommodation of seamen, which was consequently of the most primitive order.[8]

Coal is a bulky, dirty product to carry, even on the best-equipped modern steam colliers. Imagine setting out from a bleak Welsh harbour in the 1860s, in a sailing boat with 250 tons of coal in the hold, no power but what can be coaxed from the wind (which is naturally blowing cold and hard almost exactly from where you want to go). It is, of course, winter, because that is when most coal is needed (the balancing demand from industry, as we have seen, is as yet quite small). Even in the mildest weather there is the remote but terrifying possibility of the coal erupting into flames by spontaneous combustion, though statistics suggest that for small cargoes and short voyages the risk is slight. More concrete are the known dangers of the Irish coast—the regular hazards to navigation provided by wrecks gave seamen vivid reminders of how real these dangers were.

The small crew—the *North Ash* shipped six, that is, a master, a mate, three able seamen and a boy, while the *Albion* shipped eight (see Table 2.1)—struggle aloft and alow with clumsily cut canvas sails that are whipped with wicked force away from numbed hands and fingers. Subduing the sails at last, the captain sets a course and retreats below, leaving half the crew on deck. Not that there is much comfort below.

Table 2.1: *The Crew of the* Albion, *1864*

Crewman	Age	Born	Rank
John Morgans	50	Portsmouth	Master
Patrick Toole	38	Wicklow	Mate
Patrick Kearns	38	Wicklow	Able seaman
John Nowlan	28	Dublin	Able seaman
John McDowell	24	Dublin	Able seaman
Edward Morgans	16	Llanelly	Ordinary seaman
William Burn	16	Dublin	Ordinary seaman
John Toole	14	Wicklow	Ordinary seaman

Source: Returns of Crew and Voyages

The men berthed in the forecastle, a cramped and stuffy cabin which served as home also to spare anchors and paint-pots and tar casks. The appalling smell of the cable chains, stored immediately below them in the chain locker, permeated the cabin. These chains were soaked with the filth and slime of the raw sewage that permeated most rivers of the day. The men slept their watch below in hammocks, bumping against each other as the vessel moved in the wind. They served alternate watches, broken as necessary by cries of 'All hands!', when at a moment's notice they could be required to scamper up the rigging in cold and heavy winds to reduce sail.

Woe betide anyone who was slow to respond immediately. For the first offence or two his fellow crew members merely cut the hammock ropes, letting the man down with a crash as he slept. Persistent offenders might be given more drastic punishment. 'An opportunity was taken', remembered one old salt 'to reeve a rope through the lee scupper-hole and bend it to a coal basket, then slip a running bowline over the sleeper's shoulders and throw the basket into the sea, and if the vessel was going at a good speed he was quickly pulled right up to the scupper-hole, sprawling and shouting for someone to help him' as the basket threatened to pull him through the hole and out to sea.[9]

Being sailing vessels, the colliers were extremely vulnerable to weather and tide; an adverse wind might prevent any arrivals for days, but when the wind shifted, as many as forty would arrive at once at the mouth of the Liffey. A race would quickly develop, since the first in would have the choice of berth. Anyone who has experienced a crowded start in choppy conditions in one of the Dublin Bay Sailing Club's races can readily imagine the resulting collisions, and the showers of abuse as the clumsy vessels manoeuvred for advantage. If the tide was against them, the fleet would have to anchor in the bay, riding sometimes with the waves crashing over the bows until the tide changed. The voyage records of the *North Ash* in 1864 show clearly how variable the journey-time could be. The vessel made 25 journeys in that year, to and fro between Ardrossan and Dublin. The quickest journey times were three trips in May, when favourable winds allowed them to dock a day after departure. On the other hand, two trips in October and November took a fortnight each.

Once into the quays, various duties would have to be paid on ship and cargo. These came down considerably during the century, but in the 1820s colliers had to pay duties as follows:

1) Dues on landing for the improvement of the city of Dublin payable to the Wide Streets Commissioners: 11d per ton
2) Guild of Merchants dues: 6d per ton and 3s 6d per ship

3) Anchorage, slippage etc. payable to the Lord Mayor: 3s 1d per ship anchorage 1s 10d slippage per ship, 2s 3∫d for the Lord Mayor, 5s 6˜d for the Water Bailiff

4) Chapter and guild dues payable to Lord Mayor and Corporation: 1s 6d per ship annually

Assuming a cargo of 200 tons, this works out at 16d per ton, a tax of some 7.5 per cent. Dublin was, in fact, notably the dearest port in Ireland. In 1828, for instance, dues amounted to £20,000 on an import of 266,451 tons of coal; Belfast imported 129,823 tons and charged dues of £2,163.[10] Colliers were, of course, designed to sail with a heavy cargo; without that weight the vessel would float dangerously high in the water. Since it was rarely possible to arrange a return cargo, most vessels would be obliged to load up ballast, for which there was a further charge (1s 11d per ton in the 1850s), before returning to Cumberland or Wales for another load. Ballast was solid—sand or stones—not water as today. The importance of ballast in the operation of the port, in making sure that neither the gathering of the ballast nor its discharge disrupted the river banks, made the Ballast Office the natural predecessor of the Dublin Port and Docks Board.

At the beginning of the nineteenth century it is estimated that coal cost about 20 shillings a ton in Dublin and between 9 and 11 shillings in coal-producing areas; so over half the price of coal was in the transport. (Coal was actually dearer in London than in Dublin.) To bring coal inland was a further expense still—by carriage or dray it could cost 6d per ton per mile, increasing the price drastically. Twenty years later the price differential was the same, though the price in Dublin had gone down to 12 shillings.[11]

There does not seem to have been an appreciable difference between the cost of the small amount of coal mined in Ireland—in Kilkenny, Tipperary, Tyrone and the Leitrim/Sligo/Roscommon area—and imported coal. Irish coal was in awkward seams, and was always inadequate in quality and quantity to supply the growing market. For the poorer people, turf, brought to Dublin by the Grand Canal in open barges, was a possible alternative to coal. One observer noted: 'around the city and along the banks of the canal there are numerous depots for the sales of turf. It is sold retail by bulk, and the rate at which it is sold is equivalent to 10s 9d per ton.' Not only did this make it very bad value relative to coal, it was moreover 'a very inferior fuel . . . spongy and porous and damp'.[12]

As always, another alternative was to steal the coal. At an enquiry in the 1850s into the management of the port of Dublin, Thomas Ashley, a chief witness and obviously a respected figure, complained, 'there is scarcely a night in the year which passes without robberies being committed from ships in port. I think it is the duty of the Ballast Office to furnish us with at least a dozen night policemen to protect our ships.' When one witness claimed 'there was an enormous system of fraud and pilfering when unloading coals on the quay, but I think the municipal police have suppressed it.' 'Indeed,' retorted Ashley, 'I am sorry to say they have *not* suppressed it.' At this time, there were some 6,500 commercial vessels entering the Port of Dublin every year, virtually all of which were engaged in the coasting trade. Up to 200 vessels might be moored along the side of the river at any one time.[13]

Heiton and Ashley worked as coal factors and iron importers together at 13 City Quay for many years, until Thomas Heiton set himself up in his own premises in 1849, first at No. 5 City Quay and then with a partner, Gilbert Burns, in George's Quay and Poolbeg Street. It seems likely that Gilbert Burns was a sleeping partner, who provided capital to Thomas Heiton but was not otherwise involved. When Thomas Heiton died in 1877, Burns, who was also involved in the department store Todd, Burns, was still the larger contributor of capital, despite withdrawing a hefty £900 in 1876/7. There seems to have been no question of his carrying on the business himself.

The two partners started in the middle of George's Quay (opposite the Custom House) with Nos 28–31; two years later they added Nos 32 and 36. This was substantially the property that was bought with the company in 1877. In 1851 Heiton was joined by Thomas Duxbury Hewat, thereby introducing a family that has dominated the management of Heitons for several generations. Although working from different premises, it appears that the relationship between Ashley and Heiton remained close, no doubt buying consignments of coal jointly, and when Ashley retired in 1861, Thomas Heiton acquired No. 13 City Quay.

By the 1850s the focus of the coal trade had changed somewhat. In the past coal had either been bought by ship-owners from the mine and shipped at their risk, or the coal-owners themselves had shipped the coal. As we have seen, the price they got for their coal, and how long a vessel might be at the quayside selling the coal, was dependent on local conditions. As local markets matured, there was less need for either the ship-owners or the coal-owners to take this risk. In order to secure a regularity of supply (as far as wind and tide would permit), the coal merchants themselves began to charter and then to own colliers.

The Dublin-based shipping trade had gradually picked up over the previous half-century. Dublin-owned vessels imported tea direct from China (Samuel Bewley's *Hellas* bringing the first shipment two years after the East India Company's monopoly was broken in 1833). Other vessels brought timber from Canada (for T. & C. Martin), and coffee, sugar and rum from the West Indies. However, this was a temporary highlight. The West Indian trade collapsed in the 1860s, and for the following twenty years very few foreign-going vessels worked from Dublin, except for a few bringing fruit from the Mediterranean.

Virtually all the 464 ships registered in Dublin in 1854 were therefore plying the coastal trade, whether on regular routes, or as tramp coasters, picking up cargoes as they could. Of the 7,000 ships that called into Dublin in that year, 95 per cent were engaged in coastal traffic (i.e. in the Irish Sea).

The boats were mostly small, usually less than 100 tons measurement, and making numerous voyages; 130 vessels a week would call into Dublin, unload their cargo of some 250 tons and return. All this loading and unloading was, of course, done manually—Heitons, for instance, was not to invest in a steam crane until the 1880s. Only six or seven of the vessels in a week would have been bringing foreign or colonial produce. One in ten of the ships calling into Dublin were steam-driven, of which the best known would have been the passenger services, which had begun regular trips in 1820. However, steam was expensive, and for bulky non-perishable goods such as coal the economics didn't recommend themselves until much later in the century. Another famous name in the Dublin coal trade didn't move into steam colliers until the 1890s, despite having been in steam for passengers and general cargo since the 1860s. Robert Tedcastle, originally from Arran on the Solway Firth, moved to Dublin in the 1840s to represent the interests of a Cumberland colliery. He bought his first sailing collier in 1856, and continued to run them until the end of the century. For his passenger and general cargo trade, on the other hand, he bought his first steamer in 1866, and by 1897 (when his company merged with John McCormick & Co.) had three others.[14]

Apart from leases and other legal documents, the first extant record of the firm details the eleven voyages in 1853/4 of the *Albion*, in the months between 8 December 1853 and 6 September 1854. Since it was Heitons' first venture into ship-owning, there are some uncertainties in the earliest accounts as to what should be included in the voyage costs. The very first voyage, for instance, records a profit of fifty per cent of sales, but only because costs are by later standards conspicuously low.[15]

In the eleven voyages the *Albion* carried to Dublin some 2,500 tons of coal, an average of 228 tons per voyage. The coal was sold at prices ranging from 17s per ton in December 1853 to 13s in July 1854. There was also an occasional income from the sale of 'old rope' and 'old sails', but these amounted to no more than £2 in the period, just enough to pay for occasional 'assistance up river' at 12s 6d a time, when the brig was towed to the quay against contrary tide and wind.

The first cost of coal, paid to John Stanley, the supplier in Pembrey, settled down to a steady 6s per ton. Profits therefore varied according to the costs between the quayside in Wales and the customer in Dublin. Most significant of these were the payments to Captain Morgan for running the vessel. These fluctuated from £47 in February to £31 in April and July and £28 in August—perhaps the summer months would have allowed him to ship a smaller crew. Running a vessel such as the *Albion* incurred land-based costs too. The Ballast Office had to be paid 10 guineas a voyage, and there were insurance and repairs. These amounted to 10 per cent of sales. The next cost was to six or seven named individuals of smallish amounts, never more than £6 per voyage. We may presume these are sales costs, perhaps commissions of some sort.

When all this is deducted, Heiton and his partner Gilbert Burns split the profit of some 20 per cent of sales.

Table 2.2: *Breakdown of Cost of Coal*
(rounded averages for 2,512 tons over 11 voyages in 1853/4)

	£ s d	%
Heitons received	14s 5d per ton	100
Cost at Pembrey	5s 9d	40
Sailing costs	3s 2d	22
Ballast Office	1s	7
Other ship costs	4d	3
Sales costs	1s 2d	8
Profit	3s	20

Source: Heitons' Archive

In fact the eleven voyages brought the firm a total profit of £390 on sales proceeds of £1,840. This shows the cost and profit level experienced by a small shipowner and coal importer in the immediate post-Famine period. It is an account only of the coal shipped on Heitons' own vessel, for no record survives for coal shipped by Heitons on other bottoms, or for the iron side of the business.

The next record of the firm allows us an insight from another perspective. By 1872 Thomas Heiton was in his late sixties, and was at the end of his career. A surviving photograph, in his tartan plaid and tam o' shanter, shows him to be a well-set-up man, prosperously over-weight, with a patriarchal greying beard. The firm still owned only one vessel, the schooner *North Ash,* but was chartering others. A stock record dated 1 August 1872, obviously drawn up in preparation for partnership accounts, shows that on that date there were eight differ-ent vessels (including the *North Ash*) in the process of discharging coals for the firm. Discharging was a laborious process, and the ac-count records that there were 512 tons from various sources being unloaded on that day, including 156 tons of Scotch coal, 259 tons of Carlisle coal and 96 tons of Wigan coal.[16]

A list of debtors gives a profile of Heitons' customers at this date. The debtors' ledger amounted to the large sum of £9,597 (less an allowance for bad debts of £400). Creditors amounted to a mere £1,709. Of the 420 debtors, 23 per cent owed more than £20—these constituted 79 per cent of the debt.

The large debtors were mainly manufacturing organisations, of whom the largest single group was ironfounders; we have seen that ironfounders used a very significant proportion of British coal. The distillers George Roe, the department stores Todd, Burns, Pim Brothers and Brown Thomas appeared, as did paper manufacturers John McDowel & Co., Dollard and Co., and Coster Brodie. Among other well-known names of the day are a good connection with the Bewley family, including shipbuilders Bewley, Webb & Co., victuallers Bewley, Draper & Co. and sugar refiners Bewley, Moss & Co. (the first café was not to open until 1895); other names include Alex Thom the printers, the B&I Steam Packet Company, the Great Western Railway company, Alli-ance Gas, and T. & C. Martin, the timber firm. Private clients include the Earl of Longford (who owed the alarmingly high amount of £145), the Marquess of Drogheda, the Presentation Convents and many more.[17]

Five years after this record was compiled, Thomas Heiton died on 17 June 1877, aged 74. He was buried in the vault in Mount Jerome where his wife Jane had been interred fifteen years before.

Table 2.3: *Contents of Stock-in-trade 1 August 1879**

Coal	Tons	Price	Value
Scotch coal	351	12s	£211
House coal	579	15s 6d	£449
Smith's	266	13s 6d	£179
Malting	144	17s	£122
Gas	15	17s	£13
Cannell	25	25s	£35
Total	1,389	14s 6d	£1,009
Iron			
English iron	140	£5 12s	£783
Scotch iron	66	£6 15s	£448
LW iron	139	£9 10s	£1,315
Hoop iron	22	£8 0s	£179
Sheet iron	22	£8 10s	£187
Angle iron	11	£8 0s	£92
Patent rod iron	6	£12 0s	£71
Pig iron	6	£2 10s	£15
Cast steel	4	£35 0s	£132
Spring steel	8	£16 0s	£121
Cart boxes	13	£7 10s	£98
Nails, nail rods	–	–	£127
Tin			£104
Spades, kettles, pans	–	–	£39
Misc.			£142
Total			£3,853

* To simplify this table I have rounded the weights and the extensions, but not the prices: in full the first line of Iron reads: English iron 139 tons 17 cwt 1 stone 5 lb @ £5 12s = £783 3s 9d
Source: Heitons' Archive

Thomas Heiton & Co., which had grown and flourished over the years, was put up for auction. Its principal assets consisted of the schooner *North Ash*, estimated to be worth £626, its offices Nos 28–32 George's Quay, extending back to Poolbeg Street, a coal store a few doors away at 36 George's Quay, and another office on City Quay,

towards the mouth of the river. Debtors were £6,200, a salutary drop
from the level in 1872. Included in the sale was the whole stock-in-
trade of the firm, valued at £2,106 in iron and £632 in coal. There
were also seven horses, nine drays and eight weighing machines. The
business was bought for £14,450 by J. Malcolm Inglis, a Dublin businessman, and William Hewat, the nephew of Thomas Heiton's ex-
ecutor. William Hewat had previously been in the Provincial Bank,
where both his father and his uncle worked, the latter rejoicing under
the splendid title 'Chief Officer of the Establishment and Superintendent of Branches'. There was an underbid, led by Adam Winter, a
manager in the firm, and a local iron merchant called Thomas Madden. The bid was financed by McArthurs, a British iron merchant.
Given the close connection between Thomas Heiton and the Hewat
family it is not surprising that nothing came of this. *Men of Iron,* a
history of McArthurs, relates how Winter became manager (at £150 a
year) of Madden and Winter, which dealt in 'iron, coal, copper, tin-
plate, zinc, nails and other metals' as the partnership deed put it. In
1881, by which time it had ceased to trade in coal, this firm took the
name of its British parent and became Butterworth, McArthur Nash
and Co of Merchants' Quay.

Although it is easy to imagine the importation of coal and iron as a
simple trade, the complexity of the business is revealed by the detailed
listing of the stock in trade given in the balance sheet of the first year's
trading of the new partnership, dated 31 July 1878 (See Table 2.3).[18]
The 420 customers might require any one of six different types of
coal (not to mention varieties of the main categories—house coal, as
we have seen, could be sourced at several places and prices). Each of
these coal types had markedly different characteristics—steam coal,
for instance, coming in blocks much too large for a domestic hearth,
which were ignited with difficulty, but, once alight, burnt extremely
fiercely; smith's coal, on the other hand, was small and sometimes as
fine as talcum powder. These were clearly not interchangeable. On the
iron side, each iron type had its own more or less unpredictable de-

mand, for which stocks had to be kept. The relative values of stocks do not, of course, reflect the relative value of the trade. In 1896, when detailed figures first become available, total coal sales over the year were 32 times the depressed mid-summer stock level, while iron sales were only two times. If these figures were true of 1879, they would give a turnover of some £40,000 for the new partnership, of which coal would represent 80 per cent.

The two purchasers of Heitons, J. Malcolm Inglis and William Hewat, already knew the firm well. Inglis' brother Robert M. was already on the staff, and William Hewat's father Thomas had served more than seventeen years with Heitons before his death in 1868. The senior man of the two was J. Malcolm Inglis, who had been born in Dunfermline, Fifeshire in 1837 and had come over to Dublin in 1859. He was an active public figure, one of the 'great and the good' of the day, involved in numerous boards and committees. He started his public life by becoming involved in various main drainage, gas and water schemes in the 1860s, and in 1874 was elected to Blackrock Town Council. Five years later he was on the Dublin Port and Docks Board, and in 1880 he was elected a member of the Council of the Chamber of Commerce, becoming Hon. Secretary of that body in 1894 and President in 1900–2.[19] Louis Cullen, historian of the Chamber, is less than enthusiastic about Inglis' 'old style' complacency in the running of the Chamber, and, describing his time in office, writes: 'the image of the Chamber was at this stage at a low ebb'.[20] However that might be, Sir Malcolm was an active member of numerous other boards and committees, and when he died in 1902, *The Irish Times,* in a lengthy obituary, described his as 'a long, useful and honoured career'.

William Hewat, born in Dublin in 1843, was much less involved in public affairs, and it is likely that the main governance of the firm devolved on him. This relationship was crystallised in 1896 when Heitons became a limited company, and he became Managing Director and Malcolm Inglis, Chairman. The purchase of the old firm was financed by the partners putting up £4,500 capital each and borrowing the rest from the Royal Bank. According to the partnership agreement, which was eventually signed in July 1878, 'the business of the firm shall be managed and conducted by the [partners] jointly as they may arrange, and they shall each give to the business their whole and undivided time and shall each receive for such time and attention a salary of one hundred and twenty-five pounds a quarter'. As well as this £500 a year they were to get 5 per cent per annum interest on their capital (£225 a year), plus a half-share in any profits. At 35, therefore, William Hewat was being paid a very comfortable but not princely salary of £725 a year plus a share in profits. By way of comparison, Charles Eason, the head of Easons, had some £1,800 a year, and the head of the largest department of that firm got £600. One of Heitons' draymen might get £50 a year.

The accounts of the first two years of the partnership showed slight losses. However, this trend was quickly reversed, and in 1880 the two partners split a profit of £673. The following year the profit shot up to £1,492, and the partners began to re-invest in the business. In 1882 the steamer *Arbutus* (built in 1880), the barque *Eglantine* (also 1880) and the steamer *St Kevin* (1883) brought the fleet to four, with the *North Ash*. As we have seen, Heitons was the first Dublin firm of merchants to use steam for importing coal. In fact, the barque *Eglantine*, which cost £1,000, was the last sailing vessel the firm bought.

As well as vessels, the annual balance sheets show constant investment into the firm. Every year money was invested in the premises,

Table 2.4: *Distributed Profits (Loss) and Assets 1878–95*

	Assets	Profits*	%
1878	£16,783	(£588)	(3.5)
1880	£20,612	£673	3.2
1885	£36,060	£1,574	4.4
1890	£51,180	£5,822	11.4
1895	£41,817	£3,689	8.8

*Profits defined as the sums distributed to the two partners.
Source: Heitons' Archive: Voyage Book

with sums of over £1,000 being spent in 1883, in 1884, in 1888/9 and in 1895. In 1886 a steam crane appears for the first time; this cost £770, and a further sum of £800 was spent on cranes in 1890. By 1896 the firm had four steam cranes in Custom House dock. There was also a gas engine, used for cutting hay, in the stables. In 1889 the steamer *St Margaret* was added to the fleet, and the following year the *St Kilda*. The *St Margaret* eventually foundered in 1919 off Hook Point and was lost with all hands. The *St Kilda* was sold in 1898.

At this time the firm delegated the management of the small fleet to the shipbroker and agent Robert Harper in Glasgow. This development was motivated by various considerations. No doubt repair and maintenance for the steamers, which were built on the Clyde, were better in Glasgow, but also it is clear from later records that as much as a quarter of the income earned by, for instance, the *St Margaret* in 1902, was from carrying goods for firms other than Heitons. No doubt this work was more readily sourced in Glasgow.

Profits for 1882 were £2,468, of which the partners ploughed back £2,000. In 1884 profits dipped to a mere £562, but by 1887 they were back to £2,758, and they never looked back. The best year of the partnership was 1889/90. The balance sheet covering the year to 31 July 1890, as usual written in J. Malcolm Inglis' hand, shows profit of £5,822 on a total asset value of £51,180 (see Table 2.4). The business had come a long way in the thirteen years since the two men had bought it. At over £3,000 a year each, the two partners were now among the top earners in the city. The most successful barristers might hope for £5,000 a year, but the top civil servant in the country, the Under Secretary, had a mere £2,000. For the next few years profits ran at between £3,000 and £4,500.

By the middle of the 1890s Heitons was one of the leading coal-importing firms in the country. The firm was now importing more than 150,000 tons of coal a year, not to mention its extensive iron business. The growing prosperity of the country in the late 1880s had stimulated many companies to establish a firmer basis for expansion

by becoming limited corporations. Among those to go public in the
1890s were Alex Thom, Switzers, William Martin Murphy's recon-
structed Dublin United Tramway Co., and numerous others. The
quoted capital on the Dublin Stock Exchange more than doubled,
going from £7.25m at the beginning of the decade to £17.2m at the
end.

In 1896, at a high point in its prosperity, Heitons also became a
limited company, as we shall see in Chapter 3.

Chapter 3
The First Years of the Public Company 1896–1910

FOR THE WELL-OFF, Ireland was a comfortable place to live at the end of the nineteenth century. It has been estimated that earnings per capita put southern Ireland among the top fifteen richest countries in the world, richer than Norway, Spain, Italy or Japan. Of course the population— then 4.7 million, of which three-quarters were Catholic—was very much divided into the haves and the have-nots. At the top end were families on incomes of £400 or more, a sum described, with a typical touch of exaggeration, by Maurice Healy as 'untold wealth in prewar southern Ireland'.[1] On this one could happily hunt or keep a yacht in Dublin Bay. £400 is equivalent to a *take-home* pay of about £25,000 in 1995. At the other end of the scale there were labourers' families in Dublin trying to live on 15s a week, paying 2s 6d rent for a single room in a tenement. These families, in their desperation, were to precipitate the most dramatic public event that Heitons was ever directly involved in, the 1913 lockout.

Socially, Ireland was changing profoundly. Although we are accustomed to pride ourselves on living in an era of unprecedented change, there is a case to be made that the period between 1880 and 1910, a period of prosperity for Heitons, saw more fundamental changes than any similarly short period since. The rapid travelling, mass communication society tempered by intense state involvement in daily life that we live in today was born in this period. Just to list the changes and inventions that came on stream in this period makes the point. There were the motor car and the telephone—by 1911 the instrument had become relatively commonplace, evidenced by the fact that Miss Dowling, Heitons' telephone operator in Westmoreland Street, was paid 19s 10d a week, a clerk's, not a specialist's, wage. To give ordinary people mobility there was the popular safety bicycle—in 1904 the board of Heitons provided its travelling salesman, Mr Reid, with a bicycle 'to be used by office staff for business purposes'.[2] Also new to this period were social welfare (old age pensions, national insurance), mass newspaper readership, branded grocery goods, Edisons' light-bulbs and the electric power stations to go with them, electric motors and, last but not least, the Dublin Horse Show (first held in Ballsbridge, 1881). The effect of other developments, such as the commitment to oil by the British and German navies, the Panama Canal, Picasso's cubism and Einstein's general theory of relativity, were to take longer.

Although Dublin was still the centre of government in Ireland, it had lost the economic race to Belfast. Fuelled by shipbuilding and linen, that city had gone from 70,000 population to 300,000 in fifty years. Dubliners sneered at it as 'a kind of third-rate Glasgow' (Page Dickinson), or as not being truly Irish at all (Bulfin), but there was no gainsaying its success. In a culture where a person's religion was a crucial badge of identity, the fact that all this success was located in the one largely Protestant part of Ireland was highly suggestive, confirming a long-held prejudice. It seemed to many that there was something in the nature of Catholicism that prevented people taking economic development seriously. As a contemporary author put it:

> in the North-Eastern Triangle of Ireland, you find the Irishman in whose mind 'this world' is the predominant fact; but who does not by any means lose sight of the good things promised after death. In the rest of the country, you have the Irishman for whom 'the next world' is the predominant fact; and who alas often loses sight of the opportunities afforded by 'this world'; like his countryman Burke, perhaps, 'too fond of the right to pursue the expedient'.[3]

No one is wholly free of the prejudices of one's caste and class—

how far these prejudices affected daily dealings in firms such as Heitons, Easons, Jacobs, Bewleys and so on, headed by Protestants and largely staffed by Catholics, is quite unrecoverable.

In Dublin there were two groups of leaders who had little to do with each other. Since the 1880s the Corporation had been completely dominated by Catholic nationalists, mostly publicans and small merchants. As a body it was felt to be at least self-serving, if not actively corrupt. Many Protestants had retreated to the self-governing townships beyond the canals—to Rathgar and Rathmines, Blackrock, Pembroke and Drumcondra. By 1891 30 per cent of Dubliners lived outside the writ of the Corporation.

Economically the city was dominated by Protestant businesses such as Guinness, Jacobs, Jamesons, Pims, Bewleys and Findlaters. Banks and insurance companies were usually run by Protestants. There were, of course, Catholic businessmen, of whom by far the most prominent was William Martin Murphy, who owned the Dublin Tramways, Clerys, the *Irish Independent* and the *Herald*. As the Dubliners joked: 'Says the Herald: "Go to Clery's", and the trams are waiting there to take them to Clery's, so to Clery's they go and spend all their money, and 'tis Murphy has it.'[4] In a world where, at least until the 1960s, every firm was known to be either Catholic or Protestant, Heitons was clearly Protestant.

The Prospectus for Heitons' incorporation in 1896 noted how the rapid development of the business established by Thomas Heiton and Gilbert Burns had been accelerated by the general application of steam and other labour-saving appliances. The fifty-year-old firm, as the Prospectus put it:

> now ranks as one of the largest, if not the largest of its kind in Ireland. It possesses valuable and exclusive agencies, and the clientele of the house is a very extensive one, including most of the public bodies and largest consumers in Dublin and district; an extensive and valuable provincial connection is also attached and a very large trade is done direct with householders.

Coal was landed at the extensive wharfage in Custom House dock, complete with four steam cranes capable of discharging 2,000 tons of coal a day. (In a city which depended so much on casual labour from the docks, this increasing mechanisation of the loading and unloading processes must have severely reduced general employment opportunities.) The other premises now consisted of Nos. 24–32 and 36–7 George's Quay, a similar spread in Townsend Street, and a Head Office in Westmoreland Street. In 1898 a branch office was established in Cumberland Street, Kingstown (Dún Laoghaire), taking over bankrupt premises. This experiment was a success, and in 1904 a further branch was established in Bray.

As well as these land-based assets, the firm now ran, from Glasgow, a fleet of four colliers: the *St Margaret* and the *St Kilda*, with a carrying capacity of 550 tons each, and the *St Mirren* and the *St Olaf*, with a carrying capacity of some 600 tons each. 'During the summer season', noted the Prospectus, 'such of the fleet as are not carrying the company's own coal will be placed at the disposal of other shippers and no difficulty is experienced in keeping ships of this class fully and profitably occupied at all seasons of the year.'

Craig Gardner—still incidentally the firm's auditors—certified the accounts, vouching for an average annual profit of £10,873 over the previous six years. As was then the practice, this profit was calculated without taking into account depreciation, interest, or the salaries of the partners. One substantial set of figures the accountants did vouch, however, was the remarkable increase in the amount of coal imported by the firm. In the year ended 31 July 1890 it had been 105,578 tons. The following year was hit by strikes, as the coal labourers attempted to gain recognition, and the increase was small. In the year ending 31 July 1895 the firm shipped the remarkable quantity of 158,000 tons, rather more than 15 per cent of the total Dublin importation. This growth tempted the partners to overvalue the goodwill of the company: the new shareholders paid £130,000 for physical assets valued in the 1895 balance sheet at £72,000. Correcting this over-valuation was to cause the next generation some effort.

Becoming a limited company in 1896 was not quite the routine business it is today. In his *Directory of Irish Limited Companies* published in 1901 the accountant Michael Crowley noted that there were a mere 1,120 companies in Ireland, of which the great majority were northern linen concerns. There was still a faint suspicion in conservative business circles that limitation of liability was tantamount to a declaration that one could not be relied on to pay one's debts.

One common reason for incorporation of established businesses was to prepare for the death or departure of one or more of the founding partners. If a partner were to die in office, his estate would be entitled to withdraw his holding, with potentially damaging effects on the business. Heitons had seen something of this when Thomas Heiton died in 1877, and the business had in effect to be completely refinanced. Incorporation allowed for more orderly handover to the next generation.

By the mid-1890s William Hewat and J. Malcolm Inglis were in their early and late fifties respectively. Perhaps they wanted to prepare for the possibility of eventual retirement. They were both well off, with interests outside the business: Hewat was deeply involved in the Presbyterian Association, and Inglis had his finger in many pies. If they also felt the shadow of the wings of death, this was prophetic, for by 1902 both were dead.

The structure of the new firm was straightforward. Its six-member board consisted first of all of Malcolm Inglis as Chairman and William Hewat as Managing Director. These two retained 11,194 of the 12,000 ordinary shares in their own hands. Robert Harper of Glasgow looked after the Shipping Department and Robert M. Inglis continued to look after the Iron Department. Two non-executive directors were appointed, Frederick W. Pim and George Macnie: Pim was a member of the well-known Quaker business family, whose best-known venture was the department store on George's Street and Macnie was a shipowner who became Chairman of the Dublin Port and Docks

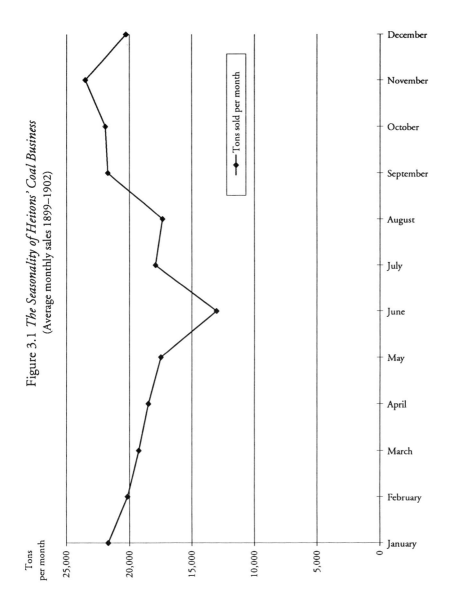

Figure 3.1 *The Seasonality of Heitons' Coal Business*
(Average monthly sales 1899–1902)

Board in 1907.

The deaths within two years of the turn of the century of the driving forces behind the company since 1877 marked the end of an era. The first to go was William Hewat, whose long-drawn-out illness—described as 'a species of paralysis'— began in the summer of 1900. The last board meeting he attended was in June of that year. He wrote to the board in September, formally notifying them, 'as my illness, while progressing favourably, promises only a slow recovery, it would much oblige me your granting leave of absence until such time as possible for me to resume work. I need hardly state that I feel my enforced idleness very keenly.' The board immediately expressed 'their great regret for his illness and their sincere hope for his speedy restoration to perfect health'.

Life had to go on. Sir Malcolm was appointed Managing Director pro tem, and William Hewat junior, his namesake's nephew, General Manager. A few months later, on 12 December 1900, the minutes recorded the board's 'deep sense of the loss which the company has sustained in the death of Mr. William Hewat . . . and of the personal sorrow for the loss of a friend with whom they had been so pleasantly associated'. His obituary (in *The Irish Times* of 7 December 1900), records his special interest in St Andrews College, of which he was one of the trustees, and his presidency of the Presbyterian Association.

In January 1901 William Hewat junior was appointed Assistant Managing Director to Sir Malcolm, a post which quickly became sole Managing Director. In March 1902 Sir J. Malcolm Inglis attended his last board meeting, and on 29 April the board 'deeply regretted to record the death of Sir Malcolm who was long identified with the interests of this company, and desire to express to Lady Inglis and her family their sincere sympathy with them in their great bereavement', a tribute notably less warm than that given to William Hewat. This may merely mean that the earlier tribute was drafted by Sir Malcolm for his long-standing partner. On the other hand, there was no mention in the minutes of the closure of the office for the funeral or the

Table 3.1: *Income and Expenditure of the Business in 1901*

	£	£	% of Sales
Income			
Sales Coal	119,473		(95)
Iron	6,180		(5)
		125,653	(100)
Costs			
First cost (purchases)			
Coal	81,390		(65)
Iron	4,966		(4)
		86,356	(69)
Sales *less* first cost		39,297	(31)
Other costs			
Freight	9,464		(8)
Wages & salaries	15,038		(12)
Stabling etc	3,123		(2)
Other costs	2,278		(2)
Total costs		29,903	(24)
Trading profit		9,394	(7)
Other income		1,361	(1)
Total profit		10,755	(8)
Distribution			
Depreciation, reserve a/cs		1,855	(1)
Distributed to shareholders			
Preference shares		3,500	(3)
Ordinary shares		5,400	(4)
Source: Heitons' Archive			

bonus of 4s a head for all weekly-paid staff voted after William Hewat's death. Sir Malcolm's obituary (*The Irish Times* 25 April 1902) recorded his many committees and interests, including his staunch Liberal Unionism.

Although the death of the two partners marked a notable change at the head of the company, placing William Hewat II in a position he was to occupy for the next thirty-five years, and elevating George Macnie to the chairmanship, there was little difference in day-to-day progress. From the accounts in the general ledger we can construct a picture of how the business ran at this time. Unfortunately, the complex way the account books are structured, and the disappearance of the backing ledgers, forces an element of reconstruction on the historian. In order to monitor the profitability of each section of the business, each of the three departments (coal, iron and shipping) had its own profit and loss account, and the profits were then transferred to a general P&L account. Without the backing information, the exact detail of the overall business in Table 3.1 must therefore remain somewhat conjectural. It is clear, however, that sales of coal and iron in that year came to £125,653—95 per cent of which derived from coal sales. This represents a turnover of some £8 million in 1996 terms. Costs stemmed basically from purchases of coal and iron in Britain, shipping and sales (see Table 3.1). The net profit available for distribution is also clear, though there was no systematic deduction for depreciation; in 1901 £1,600 was set aside for this purpose, to bring the reserve fund up to the round sum of £22,000. The 'Other income'—some £90,000 in 1995 terms—came from investments and rents (including £166 a year from tenements in Poolbeg Street). The summary shows the basic structure of the business.

Clearly the greatest cost was in the purchase of coal and iron. As a trading company, whether in coal, steel or builders' supplies, Heitons have been price-finders rather than price-makers. Despite canny buying and discounts for quantity, this remains true today. The firm was very much a price-taker in coal. All Irish imported coal came from Britain, whose output in 1901 was 219 million tons. Ireland imported some 4 million tons every year, of which 1 million came into Dublin. Heitons bought 136,000 tons—a respectable purchase quantity, but not sufficient to affect the basic economics of coal production.

The key cost variables under the company's control were therefore freight, stabling charges and wages. Operationally, there were three separate but connected businesses—shipping, coal and iron. The Shipping Department was run by Robert Harper from Glasgow. He was responsible for ensuring that the three vessels were kept in good repair and in cargo. This involved paying the crew and port charges, as well as organising the appropriate loading. Only 71 per cent of the freight charged was carried for Heitons itself, the rest was for other firms, on such random coasting errands as carrying strawberries from Wexford to Dublin, or potatoes to France. There was also coal brought in on other bottoms: for instance the *SS Mourne*, which sank in the Bristol Channel in 1899, was carrying coal for Heitons at the time.

The steam ships were surprisingly vulnerable: they were regularly reported as being in collision either with other ships or with piers and dock fittings—worse, they sank, often dragging crew members with them. For instance in January 1898 the *St Olaf* damaged herself against a quay wall and had to be sent to Glasgow to be repaired; in February 1899, the *St Mirren*, leaving Custom House Dock, damaged her stern by striking against the pier head and she also had to retreat to Glasgow. All the vessels in operation in 1896 eventually sank: the *St. Olaf* in 1900, the *St Kilda* in 1901, the *St Margaret* in 1919 and the *St Mirren* in 1926. Many crewmen died in these accidents.

Reports of damage were a regular item in the board minutes. In May 1906 the *St Margaret* was damaged in Whitehaven. In March 1907 damage was reported to both the *St Kevin* and the *St Mirren*; in May 1908 the *St Mungo* was in collision with *SS Dolores* in Dublin Bay. The *St Patrick* was involved in a collision in the Manchester Ship Canal in October 1909, before being lost at sea with the death of her captain and four crew in 1912. The following year the *St Mirren* was in collision with another vessel in Dublin, and the *St Mungo* broke down in mid-channel between Maryport and Dublin. The *St Mungo* was sunk in 1917 by German naval action, with twelve hands lost. Occasionally the company could gain by the dangers of the sea—in November 1903, the Managing Director reported salvage of the *SS Flandria* on 28 October by the captain and crew of the newly commissioned *St Patrick*. A couple of months later the Admiralty Court awarded the company £675 and the master and crew £225 for this act of bravery.

Despite this toll of damage, the fleet managed to import a formidable amount of coal. In 1901 the firm imported 136,000 tons of coal and £4,300 worth of iron. A picture of the day-to-day operation of the business in the early 1900s emerges from a little booklet produced by the company called *The History of a Black Diamond.* This traces the connection between 'the homely scuttle of coal at the side of the hearth and the luxurious vegetation of a mighty primeval forest', describing how seams of coal were deposited and eventually dug up. The booklet goes on to detail what happened to the 'Black Diamond' once it reached the surface. The coals are first screened, in a tall tower, with

a rapidly moving steel cylinder perforated like a riddle . . . the cylinder is divided into sections, the perforations of each differing in size, and running from ˘ inch at the top to 1° inch in diameter at the bottom. Thus the coal passing through the hollow of the cylinder from above downwards is thoroughly screened or riddled of all 'slack' and fine coal, and passing out at the lower end, is deposited upon a revolving steel platform, along which the coal is carried and passed before a double line of girls and boys whose business it is to pick out all foreign matter such as roofing, stones etc., and to break the large coal into convenient sizes.

The small coals are washed, and then riddled again, to emerge as one of the numerous varieties of small coals—'Gum or fine slack, Peas, Single Nuts, Double Nuts and Treble Nuts'—all of which had their own markets and uses.

At the dockyard

the quay is laden from end to end by wagons of coal and situated at regular intervals are the huge cranes by which the Black Diamond is transferred to the ship's hold. The wagons are run into large cradles, by means of which they are swung over the vessel, and the end of the wagon being removed and the cradle slightly tilted, the contents are deposited in the hold below; and so wagon after wagon, the work goes merrily on at the rate of from 100 to 150 tons per hour.

The larger of the 'Saints', the *St Mirren* and *St Olaf,* carried 650 tons, and so would be filled in under six hours. In some ports, the coal would be lifted from the wagons on to a large elevator, with a chute which directed the coal into the hold.

Arriving in the Liffey, the vessel enters Custom House docks.

Hardly is she alongside when the fillers, shovels in hand, scramble aboard. The powerful steam cranes are throbbing and vibrating as if anxious to get to work. The steamer is made fast and the signal given, the great tubs, with a capacity of 1° tons each, are swung on board and the work of discharge commences. Should we return seven or eight hours later, we would find the steamer's holds empty, and all silence and darkness.

Next morning the business of getting the coal to market commences immediately.

We arrive a few minutes before six, to find 80 horses and drays and about 160 men quietly waiting for the day's work to commence. At the stroke of six, the weighbridge having been adjusted, the first horse and dray draws on to it to be 'tared' [the dray was weighed unloaded first so that its weight could be later subtracted from the loaded weight]. Every 35 seconds sees another of the long line over the scales (driver with loading docket in hand) to its allocated place for filling the particular coal desired. Each kind of coal is under the supervision of a thoroughly competent foreman, whose sole duty it is to see that it is again 'picked' and 'screened' before being loaded . . . the loading of a ton of Black Diamond is only the work of a few minutes, so that long before the last of the incoming empty drays has been weighed, another long line of loaded ones is being formed, ready again to pass over the weighbridge the minute it is available. Very careful note is kept of all details, such as the numbers of the drivers, fillers etc., thus enabling the firm to trace any error or carelessness to the responsible person or persons.

When the breakfast bell rings at 8 am the long line of loaded and weighed drays is safely on its way, part going north, part south, part east, part west, carrying comfort to many homes.

As well as these direct sales, a relatively small amount was also sold through branch outlets in Kingstown (from 1898) and Bray (from 1904). In 1902 Custom House Dock sold 132,500 tons and Kings-

Table 3.2: *Elements of Wages Costs 1901*

	£	%
Ships' crew (including captains)	3,967	26
Dischargers (casual dock labour)	2,640	18
Fillers (filling bags inshore)	2,265	15
Draymen	3,163	21
Salaried staff	3,003	20
Total	15,038	100

Source: Heitons' Archive

town sold 8,000 tons.

Unfortunately no definitive list survives of the workforce required to process this enormous amount of coal. However, we can identify the various elements of wages costs. Many of these employees, especially the dockers working to discharge the boats, would be casual, often picked by a foreman from a large crowd to work by the day as the necessities required. This system of casual labour was to last a very long time. The seamen would be more permanent, especially those occupying posts of responsibility. It is unlikely that they were paid more than £2 or £3 a month all found.[5] The fillers and draymen would probably be paid between £1 and £2 a week. We can guess that the total full-time equivalent number of men paid wages was over two hundred.

The main burden of wages' costs was incurred in the process so vividly described in *The History of a Black Diamond* with over half going on discharging, filling bags and on draymen. Ships' crews took a further quarter, while salaried staff, including managers, sales and accounts clerks (who would tend to be better paid on average) accounted for only one-fifth of the annual wages bill (see Table 3.2). Because wages loomed so large in their costs, Heitons and other coal merchants tended to take a tough line on labour matters. This approach can seem harsh to modern eyes, but it is important to be aware of the background.

Dublin has had a long and disturbed history of industrial relations. In the early nineteenth century, when most employers were small and vulnerable, and public policing weak, skilled and unskilled workers combined successfully to enforce numerous restrictive regulations. One witness to the 1837 *Select Committee on Combinations of Workmen* told how 'on the quays of Dublin . . . among the draymen and coalporters, they would not allow any man to be dismissed from his employment, or at least if they were put out no one else went in their place, and if they did they were beaten'.

The beatings were organised by the shadowy Welters society, which was credited with various atrocities, such as vitriol throwing, burning wood yards and punishment beatings of various sorts, including most spectacularly the murder in 1829 of Thomas Hanlon, who was set on in broad daylight; half an hour later, suspecting he was not dead, the men returned and finished the job. The thirty or so men who carried out this attack were apparently picked by lot and primed with alcohol beforehand. Four of them were subsequently executed.

A favourite tactic, as in rural areas, was the despatch of anonymous threatening letters. In 1828 a Mr Murray claimed he had received this:

> Do not for a moment harbour to yourself that you are all safe because we have not interfered with you this time Back; we are determined to make you a victim, like some others before new year, if you do not employ all Irish and no Scotch, and give full wages and also discharge Bloody Red nose drinking Graham. We will pin him some night going home, unless he quits your employment, we are not to be trifled with, we are determined to do our duty. We hope, for your family's sake, that this will be a sufficient warning.
>
> Billy Welters

The hypocrisy of the last sentence has a joltingly familiar ring. Murray's house had been burned down the day before this was received.

In the skilled trades such as the shipwrights, a web of restrictions on the number of apprentices, on wage rates and on the strict separation of tasks (canal-boat carpenters not to work in the docks etc.) was widely held to have caused the decline of the Dublin shipbuilding industry, which was overtaken first by Cork and then more permanently by

Belfast. We have seen that Heitons ran its fleet of steam vessels from Glasgow largely to gain access to adequate repair and maintenance facilities.

By the end of the nineteenth century, the gradual decline of Dublin's manufacturing base and the slow mechanisation of the docks had squeezed more and more labourers into hunting for fewer jobs. In these conditions it is not surprising that militancy grew apace. Prompted by the Liverpool-based National Union of Dock Labourers, an increasing series of disputes festered from 1890 onwards. A Coal Masters Association was formed in the early 1890s, but seems to have fallen apart. However, by 1898 the board minutes noted (10 August), 'Mr Hewat reported that efforts were being made to amalgamate the Trade for mutual protection against encroachment by men.' Despite serious doubts, for the meeting was twice reconvened for 'further consideration', obviously these discussions were fruitful, for the board minutes record in July 1899 'some friction having arisen with men engaged in discharge of steamers, the matter in dispute is referred to Coal Masters Association'.

At the board meeting of 1 August 1900, it was reported that

> the labourers in the Company's employ had all gone out on 'strike' on 6 July causing considerable inconvenience through stoppage of work. Steps were immediately taken, in conjunction with the other coal merchants affected, to get in outside labour and during the strike work was as far as possible carried on. Men seeing the hopelessness of their position offered to return to work on the old terms, or on any terms on 16 July and a certain number of the old hands were taken back, a considerable number were not. The Board were pleased to learn that the result was entirely in their favour.

The next chapter will describe the most memorable of these disputes, one in which William Hewat and Heitons took a prominent part.

Strikes and disputes of this kind did not, of course, affect the salaried staff working in the accounts department and the sales offices. We can put names and memories to a few of the stalwarts. At the top was William Hewat, Managing Director, on a salary of £500 a year.

Other salaries included Robert Harper, the ship agent in Glasgow, £600, R. M. Inglis, who had been with the firm since Thomas Heiton's day and now ran the Iron Department and stables, £500; V. D. Inglis, the Company Secretary £500; in 1909 Vivian Inglis resigned and went to Australia after getting into financial difficulties.

Other names included James J. O Giollagain (Assistant Secretary) who had £195 a year in October 1907.[6] He later became manager of the Dún Laoghaire branch (incidentally the only one whose name was spelt even remotely in the Irish manner). Hamilton Whiteside, one of the firm's great characters for thirty years, became Assistant to the Managing Director in 1906 on £136 a year.[7] In April 1911 he was given a bonus of £25 on getting married,[8] and his salary was raised to £200; he became General Manager of the coal business on £250 a year,[9] and eventually joined the board. J. Denham Macalister, then a cashier, had £90 a year; during the First World War he went to fight in the trenches, but returned to the firm at the end of the war, eventually becoming Company Secretary. Less familiar names include Mr Leeson, Inspector of Branches, with £124, Mr Plumer, manager of the Spencer Dock operation, £130 a year, Charles Boyle, Junior Clerk, £45 a year.[10] An unnamed junior clerical staff member (male) got £35, and a junior clerical staff member (female) only £26. The office porter got £1 a week.

The horses and stables were a key part of the operation, costing more every year than the entire salaried staff. Most of the horses and drays belonged to Heitons. In the inventory at 1 August 1901 the firm owned 55 dray horses and mules and 12 wagon horses. There were 70 sets of harnesses, 69 drays, 15 wagons and 2 box carts. It is difficult for us, familiar only with the gaunt impersonality of a fleet of lorries, to envisage the working life of the stables as part of a day-to-day business. Each of the seventy or so animals' personality and preferences—cranky or docile, greedy or stupid, curious or vicious—would be intimately known and approved or feared by the stablemen. The clouds of warm breath of a cold morning, the clumsy and sometimes dangerous bodies, the constant smell of hay and dung and bran are lost in the mists of time. Perhaps the zoo is the nearest we can get.

A close eye was kept on the cost of maintaining this elaborate establishment. During the year ending 1 August 1901 the average of 78 horses consumed over 200 tons of hay, 40 tons of bedding, 33 tons of bran etc.[11] It was calculated that each horse cost £28 a year to maintain (some £2,000 in 1995 values). A special gas powered machine was used to cut up all this hay. It was obviously quite dangerous: Robert Inglis reported to the board 'that one of the stablemen had met with an accident involving the loss of his right arm through his hand getting caught in the hay cutting machine, which the Board heard with regret'.[12]

Looking back over his stewardship of the company twenty years later, William Hewat summarised his feelings about the task as he saw it:

at the time the company was formed, we were going through a period of good trade with substantial profits, and in the share capital was included a very substantial sum for the goodwill of the business . . . I became sole managing director on the death of Sir Malcolm Inglis. During the years that followed I was faced with unsatisfactory trade conditions, and having to recognise that the capital of the company was excessive. Over the whole period since my principal aim has been to set aside out of profits sufficient sums that in addition to developing the business would in time wipe off anything from the balance sheet that could possibly figure under the heading of 'Goodwill'.

This concern with 'balance-sheet rectitude' was also felt by William Hewat's contemporary, Alexander Nesbitt of Arnotts. In the manner of their day, both men looked askance at the optimism of their predecessors. In Arnotts' case the flotation of the company in buoyant trading conditions in the 1870s had encouraged the promoters to inflate the share value. It took two generations of steady work to reduce the goodwill on Arnotts' balance sheet to a value the management felt happy with.[13]

Hand in hand with this concern about goodwill went a conservative valuation of assets. As William Hewat wrote with pride in 1920, 'looking at the items such as steamers, steam cranes, motors, horses, etc., these stand in our Balance Sheet at considerably under their value if put up for sale'. It is a matter for speculation how far this deeply pessimistic concern with the break-up value of the company injured it by inhibiting investment, or on the contrary strengthened it appropriately for the rougher times to come.

Chapter 4
The Glare of Public Limelight
1910–1920

BY 1910 HEITONS HAD ACHIEVED an enviable position in the Dublin business world. Its 45-year-old Managing Director, William Hewat, was a respected figure in the city, soon to be elected Chairman of the Port and Docks Board. From the constant mention of his name, and the prominent position Heitons took, William Hewat was clearly an important actor both in the Coal Merchants Association and in the Employers Federation. His election to the board of the Dublin Tramway Company (in 1916) and the presidency of the Dublin Chamber of Commerce in the troubled year of 1922 suggests that his leadership was appreciated by his fellow businessmen. In 1923 he was one of five Dubliners proposed by the Dublin Businessmen's Association to stand for the Dáil. He was one of two who won a seat, remaining as a representative for Dublin North until 1927.

The firm's strategy of constant investment in machinery and equipment was paying off, as was its new policy of developing sales depots outside Dublin—Kingstown, Bray, Howth and eventually Newbridge. At the same time an elaborate accounting system which treated each branch and activity as a separate profit centre enabled the managing director to keep a very close eye on profitability. A highly motivated and loyal staff, proud of the firm's history and importance to the local economy, kept standards high.

The firm had three significant sources of income. By far the largest,

Table 4.1: *Income by Source (Year Ending 31 July 1910)*

	£	£	%
Coal sales			
Custom House Dock	£65,138		
Spencer Dock	£36,105		
Kingstown (Dun Laoghaire)	£9,893		
Bray	£3,893		
Total coal sales		£115,029	81
Earnings carrying freight for other companies			
St Margaret	£4,068		
St Kevin	£6,921		
St Mungo	£625		
St Mirren	£5,198		
St Patrick	£5,181		
Total freight for other companies		£21,993	15
Sales of iron, cement, timber etc.			
George's Quay	£3,289		
Kingstown	£334		
Bray	£1,678		
Total iron, etc.		£5,301	4
Total income		£142,323	100
Profit (before depreciation)		£9,271	
Profit % of sales			6.5

Source: Heitons' Archive: Private Ledger 1910

representing 81 per cent of turnover, was the sale of coal. This amounted to £115,029 (see Table 4.1). Income from freight carried for other companies was £21,993, and sales of iron, cement and timber were £5,301. The total turnover therefore was £142,323 (approximately £8.5m in 1995 terms), on which a profit of 6.5 per cent was made. There was also some income from investments, from interest and from rents. Physically the firm was bringing more than 10,000 tons of coal a month into two docks, Custom House and Spencer; two years later it began landing coal at Ringsend as well.

Coal usage had by now penetrated throughout Ireland, even to the

Table 4.2: *Consumption of Coal in 1911*

Area	Population 000	Coal (Tons) 000	Usage %	Tons per Head
Leinster	1,162	1,295	31	1.11
of which Dublin	305	683	16	2.24
Munster	1,035	762	18	0.74
of which Cork	77	201	5	2.63
Ulster	1,581	1,992	48	1.26
of which Belfast	387	879	21	2.27
Connaught	611	106	3	0.17
Total	4,390	4,155	100	0.95

Source: Irish Coal Industry Committee 1919 (Cmd 650)

depths of Somerville and Ross's West Cork—'What vile coal this is!' declared one of their characters. 'Tim says . . . the English fill the coal ships with stones for the Irish market! I really think he's right.'[1] Nonetheless there was a marked difference in usage between town and country. In the big cities—Belfast, Cork and Dublin—more than two tons a head were being burned. In Connaught, on the other hand, consumption was much less. The north's industrial prominence was vividly displayed in the fact that almost as much was burned in Ulster as in the rest of the country put together. Belfast, with only 9 per cent of the population, burned 21 per cent of the coal.

Although Dublin may have been a comfortable place for those at the top of the pile, in the rare old times it certainly was not for those anywhere near the bottom. The city was now experiencing the effects of the long trend away from manufacturing into the import and distribution of British made goods. Although people were constantly attracted into Dublin from the country, there were few jobs. Thousands relied on scanty and irregular work as general labourers, like Joxer Daly and Jack Boyle, picking up a few days work here and there. (Incidentally, according to his wife Juno, 'Captain' Boyle 'was only wanst on the wather, in an oul' collier from here to Liverpool'.) The 1911 *Census* identified 90,000 adult males living in the city, of whom 24,900 were either general labourers, carters, draymen, messengers or porters. They worked in the docks, on building sites, or lifting, carrying, carting and humping loads across the city, sometimes as permanent employees, often not, earning perhaps £1 for a long week of 70 hours of physical labour. The casual labourers' situation was typified by the 'read-out' in the docks. The stevedore from Heitons, or Tedcastles or any one of the importers who had a vessel to unload, stands on a chair; around him stand fifty or sixty men. He calls out twenty names. These are the lucky ones—the rest must look elsewhere. This was a scene, of course, repeated in dockyards throughout the world. The difference in Dublin was that, because the manufacturing base was so small, in contrast to London or Liverpool or New York, there was no way out except emigration.

The *Irish Worker* described the circumstances of one labourer's family:

> Labourer: aged 40, has wife and three children; usual earnings 15s a week; when working full time 18s a week; average weekly expenditure on food 9s 6d, rent of room 2s 6d, fuel and lighting 1s 3d. Daily dietary consists of tea, bread and butter, dripping, potatoes—bacon for husband, sometimes a little fresh meat; on Sundays pig's cheek and cabbage. Husband suffers from a delicate chest in the winter and is consequently sometimes without employment.[2]

The family lived in a single room, like one-third of families living between the canals. In the large houses, hand-me-downs from the grandees of the past whose descendants retreated first to the south of the city, then to Rathgar and Blackrock or perhaps London, every room housed a similar family. Twelve rooms might house as many as sixty people— no physical or mental privacy, every squabble or gesture of love known to the rest of the landing. Sanitary arrangements, in these houses originally erected in the eighteenth century, ranged from the primitive to the non-existent. Everyone was intensely aware always of the noise and life of ten families, their hygiene, their cooking, their sickness, their bursts of luck. For many of these families, this was an immense social prison, without the consolation of anyone taking responsibility for providing food.

The social and political problem these men and their families represented was hardly solvable by current political ideas. Rents from tenements were paid to all sorts of respectable people, including the nationalist politicians on the Corporation—even Heitons had a small income from that source. The idea that the state had a duty to organise jobs for its people was in the future. Something, it was clear, had to be done—what, and by whom, was less obvious. In his presidential address to the Chamber of Commerce in January 1913, William Martin Murphy declared that

> the insanitary surroundings of the poorer classes in this city and the conditions under which they are obliged to live cannot and should not be a matter of indifference to the commercial community. . . I would exhort employers of labour not to think that all was well and so neglect to consider with sympathy the conditions and wages of their employees, especially those in the lowest grade, who are so seriously affected by any rise in the price of food.[3]

At the start of the labour troubles of 1913 Murphy returned to the charge: 'some employers bred "Larkinism" by the neglect of their men'.[4]

The skilled unions gave no idea to ordinary working people how the great problem might be solved, neither did the church, the intellectuals, nor the political leaders of either working or employing classes. With a few exceptions, the intellectuals were absorbed in their own nationalistic dreams. Business activity, except of the most high-flown arts and crafts sort, was routinely sneered at as 'mere Manchesterism' in the earnest classrooms of the Gaelic League. Very few in the Irish Republican Brotherhood agreed with Connolly's prophetic statement that 'if you remove the English army tomorrow and hoist the green flag over Dublin Castle, unless you set about the organisation of the Socialist Republic your efforts would be in vain. England would rule you through her capitalists, through her landlords, through her financiers.'[5]

Paradoxically, ordinary unionist businessmen would be more likely to accept that view, drawing of course the different inference that Home Rule was at best an illusion, at worse an opportunity for ineffectiveness and corruption worse (and on a national scale) than that already demonstrated in Dublin Corporation. In the same article, Connolly declared that he wanted to 'destroy, root and branch, the whole brutal materialistic system of civilisation, which like the English language we have adopted as our own'. Of course, desperate men are entitled to speak desperately. The French Revolution was, after all, cosily embalmed in a hundred years of history. At this end of the twentieth century, however, the Thousand Year Reich, the Gulag Archipelago and Pol Pot have largely sated our enthusiasm for root and branch destruction of civilisations.

Into this maelstrom came the simplistic charisma of Jim Larkin. Born in Liverpool in 1876, he worked as a seaman and then as a foreman on the docks. After losing his job for leading his men out on strike, he became an organiser of the National Union of Dock Labourers, in which capacity he was active in the disturbances in Belfast in 1908. As was to happen again, his extreme militantism and casual ways with union funds embarrassed his superiors, and he was sacked in December 1908. He at once set to founding a new Irish union, which became the Irish Transport and General Workers Union.

The new union was to be an Irish version of the One Big Union American socialists dreamed about, uniting all the scattered unskilled workers on the farms, on the trams, in the docks, and throughout the city. Unity was strength—by combination the despised unskilled workers, many of whom occupied humble but crucial positions, could maximise their bargaining power. From the start the ITGWU favoured three powerful weapons. These were the sympathetic strike, the concept of tainted goods and the systematic use of verbal and physical intimidation. By ruthless use of these a strike in any part of the economy could quickly spread to the whole. In theory, every strike, arising out of whatever local grievance, could, at the bidding of Liberty Hall, instantly become general. If mutual membership of the same union didn't work, the general union appealed to fellow workers not to handle goods 'tainted' by their strike.

The disruptive potential of these weapons was immense. The entire city, from hospitals to factories, depended on coal; households got warmth and cooking either from coal directly or from coal-gas. Without refrigeration, food was bought daily, so a few days' closure of the ordinary transport systems quickly caused hardship, as the city was to discover in 1916. In his speeches William Martin Murphy often raised the spectre of 'King' Pataud, the flamboyant and irresponsible French electricians' leader, who, in the middle of a strike that had plunged Paris into darkness, received journalists in the brilliantly lit Parisian equivalent of Liberty Hall. On another occasion he got the electricians at the Opera to strike just minutes before a gala performance before a visiting royal—after a few hectic minutes of negotiation in the dark, they got their rise.[6]

Given the potential power of his union, what alarmed Larkin's opponents, including other trade union leaders, was his total disregard for the 'responsible' conventions of the day. Larkin was, for instance, characteristically blunt about agreements between workers and employers. 'To hell with contracts,' he famously said on one occasion when the moderate railway union declared it was legally obliged to transport tainted goods. In 1908 a careful structure of Conciliation and Arbitration Boards was hammered out between the employers and the National Union of Dock Labourers—William Hewat was one of the four employers' representatives at the conference in Dublin Castle. In 1911 the ITGWU took the unilateral view that an agreement of this sort was extorted from the workers under duress, and was therefore morally void. As Connolly put it in 1913, 'no Conciliation Board ever established would be able to patch up an agreement for which in the future good solid moral grounds could not be found for breaking'.[7] 'In this golden age of the agitator', writes one scholar, 'Larkin came to share syndicalism's aversion to politicians and bureaucrats, its hope for a state run by

Thomas Heiton (1804–77) as he would have looked when he set up Heitons as a separate trading company in 1849

William Hewat (1843–1900)— after employment in the Provincial Bank, he and J. Malcolm Inglis bought Thomas Heiton's business in 1877.

Thomas Heiton in old age—despite having lived in Ireland almost all his life his sentimental identification with his Scottish origins was obviously still strong.

Sir Malcolm Inglis in the official uniform of a Deputy Lieutenant of the City of Dublin.

Robert M. Inglis, who died as Company Secretary in 1923, joined the firm when Thomas Heiton was still alive. He was the first but by no means the last to achieve fifty years' service.

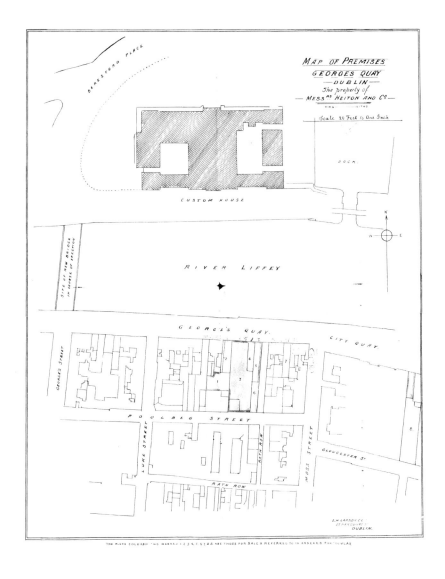

The auctioneer's map showing the George's Quay premises owned by the firm in 1877; Heitons finally vacated these premises more than a hundred years later.

17–18 Westmoreland Street, for many years the form's head office, was finally sold in 1973.

George's Quay in the 1950s

Marketing techniques: this calendar (running from October to September) was distributed to customers. In the centre was a pack of tear-off postcards by which customers could order coal to be delivered to their homes. Note the very low telephone numbers. The back contained detailed calendar and postal information such as the dates of Bank Holidays, law terms and the costs of telegrams and parcels.

Constant watch had to be kept on the quality of the coal received. Out of the mine, coal is full of slack (above)—washed and screened it looks like the best English household coal (below). Some industrial customers preferred the more powdery coal, which bulked less and was cheaper. Screening and washing could reduce a slacky heap by as much as 30 per cent. Such a heap was likely to be wasted by wind and rain.

The company began processing coal through Spencer Dock in 1904. (*Above*)
One of the company's ships having completed discharge (*Below*) Coal was
lifted straight from the hold to the top of the tower-like screening plant and
then deposited into railway waggons.

VIEW OF SCREEN WORKING.

(Above) This view of the Spencer Dock screening plant was used on a postcard for industrial ordering. The pre-printed text on the card read: 'Kindly forward to . . . station . . . waggons of . . . coal, doubled screened/ex ship.' (Below) An early Heitons lorry, registered about 1910—note the solid tyres

The second St Mungo *under construction in a small shipyard (1920)*

St Mungo *in dry dock in Birkenhead, for repairs to the starboard side after an accident (1931). The* St Mungo *was eventually broken up in 1954.*

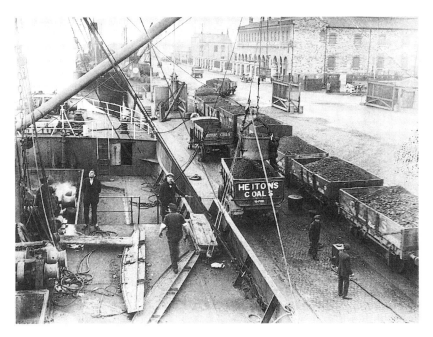

(Above) Unloading at the North Wall gates—the Point Depot is pictured on the top right. Unscreened coal is being taken from the hold by the ship's winch directly into wagons and lorries for industrial users. (Below) Heitons regularly won prizes at the RDS Spring Show for the turnout of its working horses and drays.

Office scenes: (Left) Frank Nunns and J. J. O Giollagain, who both worked for more than fifty years with the firm. Nunns retired in 1930 and O Giollagain in 1934. (Below) Head Office Accounts in 29 George's Quay (1949) (l–r) Sid Kane, Beatrice and Frances Homan, Dick Brown, Cyril Kavanagh and Kay Shanks. The large sloping desks on the right were necessary to enable the clerks to work on the enormous ledgers. A strict dress code was enforced— women wore overalls, men suits (except on Saturdays when jackets and grey trousers were allowed).

From mine to fireplace, coal absorbed an enormous amount of manual labour. (Above) These men are filling coal from the heap into sacks for domestic customers. (Middle) Loaded drays passing over the weighbridge in Custom House Dock before spreading out across town (Below) Coal being delivered to one of Dublin's opulent suburbs.

(Left) Hughie Courtney the stevedore—a noted figure on the Dublin quays. 'In those days labour disputes were often settled by strong arm methods, at which form of argument he was particularly persuasive.' (J. D. Macalister) (Below) A Heitons lorry on the weighbridge in the Bray branch under police escort in 1913

McFerran and Guilford's Tara Street premises in 1912

Tara House, the new showroom, in 1967

Telephone Nº 304 & 974

Thos. Heiton & Co. Limited.

18, Westmoreland St.

DUBLIN, 18th Aug.t 1905

Head Office.

DUBLIN :
18, Westmoreland Street.
Telephones 304 and 974.

Branch Offices.

DUBLIN :
30 & 31, George's Quay.
Telephone 1435.

KINGSTOWN :
20 & 21, Cumberland Street.
Telephone 16.

BRAY :
1, Castle Terrace, and
Meath Road.
Telephone 20.

HOUSE COALS,
STEAM COALS,
GAS COALS,
SMITHS' COAL,
ANTHRACITE COAL,
RANGE NUTS,
STEAM NUTS,
SLACK, COKE,
&c., &c.

IRON, CEMENT,
&c., &c.

WEIGHT AND QUALITY
GUARANTEED.

Dear Sir,

We have Steamers due next week to discharge direct into Railway Waggons at Whitehall the following Coals

Scotch   on Tuesday 10/5 per ton

Best Hagan   Thursday 12/9 "

5ft Orrell   " Friday 14/- " "

If open for any of these Coals we are sure we can give you every satisfaction as regards size & quality.

Looking to be favoured with your esteemed orders which shall receive our particular care & attention.

Yours faithfully
Thos. Heiton & Co. Ltd
per R.D.

Looking for business in 1905

the workers themselves, its belief in the power of the irrational, and its conviction in an alternative proletarian morality.'[8] One of the employers' most frequent claims was the impossibility of negotiating with a person holding such views.

Larkin's first task was, as he himself put it, to engender discontent among working people. Such is the resilience of the human spirit that many people living in tenements were, as one witness put it: '*extraordinarily happy* for people who were so savagely poor . . . They loved this thing, particularly the women, sitting on the steps of the tenements there on a summer's day chatting and the children running around. They *liked* that. That was the extraordinary thing, they were fulfilled.' Many other commentators spoke of the 'great number of Dubliners who are actually on the starvation line who move about with unruffled cheerfulness and good humour'.[9] A revolution required a less fatalistic attitude, and a focused hatred to provide people with the will to suffer at its behest.

The prime instrument by which discontent was to be spread was the *Irish Worker*. From its first issue in May 1911 this paper vilified the employers—'men with an income of £5,000 a month, moral lepers, men whose very breath breathed death . . . a leprous crew, the earth would be well rid of them'. The worst abused was William Martin Murphy, described in another issue as 'a creature who never hesitated to use the most foul and unscrupulous methods against any man women or child' that stood in his way, 'a soulless, money-grabbing tyrant'. With abuse came hints of violence. In July 1911 the employers' federation was warned that

these gentlemen seem to have forgotten that we had a land problem in Ireland, and that a few individuals who claimed they owned the land were taught a lesson . . . some of them found themselves lying behind a ditch suffering from want of breath. . . . Do you think there are no brains, brawn or muscle left in this land amongst the working class?

A special disgust was reserved for strike-breakers—'scabs' as the union called them, 'free labourers' in employer-speak—'a scab is a traitor to

his class, a deserter who goes over to the enemy . . . if England is justified in shooting those who desert to the enemy, we are justified in
killing a scab'. They were often denounced by name:

> we think Miss Aggie Shields of Cole Lane would be much better em-
> ployed attending to her duties for which she is engaged than acting as
> informer and tale-bearer in Jacobs Biscuit factory . . . we deal out no
> half measures to the man or woman who joins hands with an employer
> to injure other workers, so it would be as well for this young lady to
> reconsider her position.

Names and addresses of other scabs were published: 'This week we
publish the name and address of the female scabs now employed in the
Ratified Chocolate Co. [including] Maud Paily, 25 Charlemont Mall,
Annie Keegan 47 Smithfield' and 24 more. During the 1913 strike
photographs of scab labourers were displayed in the windows of
ITGWU offices.

During the next two years a series of skirmishes characterised relations between employers and the union. In August 1911 for instance,
Heitons' board minutes noted that 'the managing director reports that
any acute labour difficulties affecting the company have settled themselves for the time being, but that outlook is far from reassuring—the
loss sustained by the company from this cause has materially affected
the profits during July.'[10]

By August 1913, the air was thick with rumours of strikes and lock-
outs. Both sides, employers and workers, were girding for a fight. In
July William Martin Murphy sacked men from the *Independent* and
the Tram Company for membership of the union. Larkin asked Easons
not to sell the newspaper. When they refused, he persuaded the dock
workers to refuse to handle any goods from England addressed to
Easons. In its characteristic style the *Irish Worker* reported a meeting of
the employers on 15 August:

> It turned out a complete fiasco. The only resolution was something like
> this: 'That this meeting of the employers pledge themselves to assist
> each other by every means in their power in all labour troubles that
> may arise, if necessary to the extent of locking out their men.' T.

McCormick moved that the last sentence be deleted. This was carried. Hewat wanted to know why 'M'C' would not let the original resolution go. 'M'C' said that being a member of the shipping federation [which had a separate agreement with the union] prevented this. Hewat said this was all nonsense, as he was a shipper to the extent of sending potatoes to France occasionally . . . Hewat held forth for all he was worth to have the original resolution carried. His principal argument was how degrading it was to be dictated to by [Larkin] and that it would put an end to forever of 'do this' and 'do that' from [Larkin]. Anyhow this is all William Martin's manoeuvring has come to for the moment with Hewat as chief pawn.

The *Freeman's Journal* reported (20 August) the disconcerting possibility that the union was planning to go on strike in the middle of Horse Show Week, Dublin's international showcase. On 26 August it happened. Trams around the city stopped in their tracks, as 70 out of 200 teams of drivers and conductors got out, leaving the passengers sitting there. Murphy quickly organised scratch crews, and with some delay a curtailed service was patched together.[11] The sight of trams in operation not unnaturally infuriated the strikers and several were attacked and stoned. A series of meetings addressed by Larkin, most spectacularly in O'Connell Street, was broken up by the police. Two men died and hundreds were treated for injuries.

On 2 September Tedcastle McCormick dismissed 100 men who refused to deliver coal to a farm in Coolock, where a strike of farm labourers was in progress. The following day the Coal Merchants Association decided to lock out ITGWU men, announcing that 'union officials have declared that they will not allow deliveries to be made to any persons or firms having any dispute with them'. Over a thousand men were affected by this decision. As if to underline the workers' plight, on the same day two large tenement houses in Church Street suddenly collapsed into the street, killing three adults, two boys and two small children. Luckily it was only a quarter to nine in the evening, and most of the 46 members of the eleven families living in the houses were out and about.

On 4 September the 400 members of the employers' federation also decided to lock out ITGWU men. This was the beginning of a long series of lockouts. On 9 September a conference was held in the Shelbourne Hotel between the union and the employers, which William Hewat attended (as the representative of the Coal Merchants' Association) with William Martin Murphy and Charles Eason. After seven hours the conference adjourned, hopelessly deadlocked. The newspapers, particularly in Britain, blamed the employers for intransigence, and hard things were written about the grasping stupidity of Dublin businessmen and their willingness to let the workers starve.

By 9 September the *Freeman's Journal* reported that 'the coal trade has been almost completely disorganised by the strikes and lock-outs . . . the retail price of coal has gone to 3s per 10 stone bag, up from 1s 6d'. Naturally a few opportunists exploited the situation. Two or three small importers refused to join the lockout, and were accused of profiteering. Retailers raised their margins on coal. By 16 September there were more than 12,000 men idle, including farm-workers in north and south County Dublin. The harvest work was suspended, and milk, potatoes and vegetables were becoming scarce. Stocks of coal were estimated at less than 50,000 tons, no more than two weeks supply.

On 18 September the *Freeman's Journal* reported 'a strange quiet everywhere'. Activity in the docks was limited to one or two companies. The centre of town was also quiet, as people kept away for fear of disturbances—several trams had been attacked. 'The hum of life is concentrated around Liberty Hall. Eden Quay, Butt Bridge and Beresford Place are thickly populated all day and practically all night. It is a dull dismal crowd, enlivened only occasionally by the starting of a procession or the delivery of a speech from the windows.'

The following day the twelve members of the Coal Merchants' Association decided to pool their resources and carry on as a syndicate for the duration. The first coal delivered under the new arrangement left Heitons' stores at the Custom House Docks, under 'an imposing escort of half a dozen mounted policemen and twelve constables'. The escort was by no means symbolic: a couple of weeks later a large group of strikers caught one of Heitons' men and knocked him down and kicked him severely. On another occasion police had to disperse a crowd who followed a coal lorry hissing and booing all the way to Merrion Square.

Between September and January the union and the employers fought an increasingly bitter battle. While employers struggled to maintain a skeleton service with strike-breaking labour, incidents of violence were reported every day—everything from stone-throwing, assaults and verbal intimidation by large crowds of women and men, to the murder of two scabs, one by drowning, the other beaten to death. A policeman was nearly drowned when a group of workers threw him into the Liffey and prevented rescue attempts. Since the free workers often carried revolvers for their own safety, it was inevitable that someone would be shot: right at the end of the strike, in January 1914, Alice Brady was wounded returning from Liberty Hall with her allowance of food and died soon afterwards.

Interventions made by the British trade union movement, by government, by the Lord Mayor, by the Archbishop and by well-meaning intellectuals such as Tom Kettle and George Russell, failed to get over the fundamental points at issue. Connolly and Larkin believed that the employers had forfeited their right to control their businesses by exploiting the appalling conditions of the ordinary labourer to line their own pockets. The employers refused to deal with Larkin, who had declared in advance his refusal to be bound by agreements, and they also refused to be exposed to the constant risk of a sympathetic strike, in which their own businesses could be ruined in pursuit of a dispute elsewhere about which they could do nothing. The employment of free labourers, often industrial innocents from the West, complicated the usual post-strike issue of reinstatement. Between the combatants, the workers and their families relied on food ships from Britain. Only mutual exhaustion would bring the sides within hailing distance.

By early November a deal was in place between the shippers and the union, and the *Freeman's Journal* reported 'increased activity along the

North Wall and motor traffic has been steadily growing for the past week'. However the greater use by Guinness and other firms of imported 'free labour', many living in depot ships moored on the quays, enraged the union. On 8 November Connolly announced a programme of mass picketing. The men were to mount permanent pickets at their place of work—'men will receive food tickets from their respective Committee men, delegates or shop stewards, to whom they must report in the morning and who have the power to refuse if they consider that the member applying has neglected to attend the mass picket'. (This is one of the few glances the ordinary newspaper reader was given of the detailed organisation of the union's activities. William Martin Murphy commented that many of the returning workers declared that they hadn't known what ruthlessness was until they joined the ITGWU. A few days later Connolly announced the formation of the Irish Citizens' Army.) Despite the threats, the mass picket was not a success and it was quickly abandoned.

The union, breaking its recent agreement with the steam packet company, on the grounds that they were importing 'free labour', called dock labourers out again on 12 November. Larkin went to England to drum up British union support for the Dublin men, but although his powerful oratory and a deep sympathy for the plight of the Dublin workers generated great popular support, he managed to alienate the leaders of the British trade union movement, who refused to come out on sympathetic strike. This was the last chance. In January Larkin announced: 'We are beaten. We make no bones about it; but we are not too badly beaten still to fight.'

By March 1914 such men as the firms would re-employ had gone back to work, and William Hewat reported 'particulars and developments in connection with the strike and the final results arrived at' to the Heitons' board (incidentally the first such meeting since November 1913). One of these results was a drop in sales of perhaps £60,000 and a collapse in profits to one-third of the level of the previous year.[12] For the first time since incorporation no dividend was paid on the Ordinary shares. Expenditure on four motor cars and a tipping motor lorry

Table 4.3: *Senior Management Roles in 1914*

Head Office, 18 Westmoreland Street
Office work and general routine — *Mr O Giollagain*
General management, embracing
    town and country, oversight of docks
    and wharves etc. — *Mr Whiteside*
Secretarial work, insurances etc. stable
    department, premises — *Mr Inglis*
George's Quay
Branches Department, Iron and Accessories,
    Bray, Kingstown, Newbridge and Naas,
    also Motors Department — *Mr Maxwell*
Audit Department, check all returns from
    branches and generally look after returns
    from various sources — *Mr Leeson*

Source: Heitons' Archive: Staff Committee Minutes

was recorded—the carters and draymen were the last group to go back, and by the time they did many of their jobs had gone, either taken by free labourers or swept away by the introduction of motor lorries. The 'purchase jointly with T. McCormick's of a house at No. 2 Beresford Place for housing free labourers' was announced. Given that Liberty Hall was only the other side of Beresford Place, this seems a somewhat provocative gesture. The introduction of motors made the old weighbridge in the Custom House docks obsolete, and a new one was put in hand.

It seems likely that the stresses of the strike period led to the establishment of the staff committee. This was a regular meeting of the senior departmental managers whose object, as William Hewat described to the board, was 'to secure joint action in connection with the working of the different departments and the better management of the business as a whole'. It was in effect a decentralising executive committee. Hewat went on: 'what I feel we want is more initiative, and that I should be relieved of some of the burden of responsibility for the management. I feel this will be gradually attained.' One of the committee's first acts was to clarify the various responsibilities of its members (see Table 4.3)—since this quite simple structure was only agreed, as the minute puts it, 'after some discussion', the job definitions before must have been very vague.

The staff committee, which was reconstituted in 1931 as a Management Committee, dealt with typical day-to-day problems such a company throws up. A typical meeting took place on 15 November 1917: there were present Messrs Hewat (chair), O Giollagain, Leeson, Maxwell, Whiteside, and the Secretary, R. M. Inglis. Coal output data were reported for the week, the cash book was examined and cheque payments athorised. Repairs to one of the weighbridges were agreed. The managers of the Bray and Kingstown branches responded to a previous minute about trading expenses. On staff matters, the lady members were to be provided with special overalls ('Miss Searight to consult with the others'), and Miss Chipperfield was appointed at £1 a week, to be reviewed. A Mr A. W. Hewitt of D'Olier Street wrote complaining about being splashed with mud by one of the company's lorries. A mollifying letter was drafted, apologising of course, but pointing out that if the Corporation kept the streets clean such matters would not arise.

By the time the final accounts for the year ending 31 July 1914 were ready, the First World War had broken out. The first time the war appeared in the minutes, however, was a few months later when Hugh Harper, the company's shipping agent in Glasgow, applied for leave of absence for the duration, since he had accepted a commission in the Royal Engineers. He was to be joined in the forces by the Managing Director's two elder sons W. E. D. Hewat and Cecil D. Hewat, and J. Denham Macalister. Hamilton Whiteside, the General Manager, was appointed a Director in his place.

The scanty, rather formal, board minutes do not reveal much about the special difficulties of the war. The confidence in each other the employers had gained during the experience of 1913 was shown three years later when a 'strike of men discharging steamers, which had gone on from the middle of June to the beginning of August, and which,

Table 4.3: *Income from Coal Sales 1912–20*

Year to 31 July	Coal sales	Profit	Excess Profit Duty Reserve
	£	£	£
1912	144,510	16,112	
1913	163,781	12,446	
1914	137,473	4,522	
1915	224,143	18,678	
1916	260,236	24,241	7,000
1917	390,359	24,992	10,000
1918	353,457	24,745	10,000
1919	391,457	21,432	8,000
1920	530,534	40,213	16,000

Source: Heitons' Archive: Private Ledgers

through exhaustion of stocks of coal in yards had caused a secession of work, had been settled and work is now resumed. The operations were controlled on behalf of the merchants by the Coal Merchants' Association which met regularly and decided all matters arising'.[13] The Easter Rising came at a time of relatively slack demand for coal, though, not surprisingly, the staff committee minutes record a temporary hiccup in activity. For the week ending 20 April 1916 Custom House and Spencer Docks between them sold 2,631 tons of coal; there is no record for the following week, and for the week ending 5 May it was a mere 920 tons. By the next report, covering the week to 12 May, activity in the two docks was back to 2,798 tons. One W. Roache, a clerk in the George's Quay office, was reported as 'continuing absent'; the staff committee agreed that he had forfeited his job. In August he wrote to the board, but he was not re-employed. No doubt many casual workers, politicised by the events of 1913, also took part.

The inflation of the war years saw Heitons' turnover mounting and profits with it. In September 1915 the Chancellor of the Exchequer brought in a 50 per cent Excess Profits Duty, and from then until 1920 a total of £51,000 was set aside to meet the obligations under the duty.

When the final settlement of the duty was agreed in 1923, it was found that £10,000 too much had been set aside. As a result of the duty, net profits, which had been running at 7 per cent of coal sales before the war, were pegged below 5 per cent from 1917–20.

However, there was enough to indulge in some investment, and in December 1916 a plot of land was taken in Rathmines, with a view to creating a coal depot there, with a tramway connection (at the same meeting William Hewat had informed the board of his co-option as a Director of the Tramway Company.) By this time the *St Mirren* had been requisitioned by the government, leaving the *St Margaret*, the *St Kevin* and the *St Mungo* (the *St Patrick* sank in 1912).

The resumption of unrestricted submarine war by the Germans in February 1917 was quickly felt. Over 150 vessels were sunk in a four-week period. The *St Mungo* was attacked and sunk in June, with the loss of ten crew members. Now, instead of the five steamers that had carried the business in 1910, the company was attempting to do the same work with three. National coal stocks quickly ran down, and in September 1917 the board was informed of 'the general position as regards control, and the likelihood of prices being fixed'.[14] By February 1918 the Coal Controller had fixed the 'standard price of 46s 6d per ton net for standard coal'. Before the war the very highest price for a ton of coal was £1.

In March 1918 the board heard more of the 'serious position as regards future supply of coal owing to the requisition of steamers for other work and that Mr Hewat has been appointed on Committee formed covering representatives from all districts in Ireland to go into the matter'. In September 1918 (with the war still dragging out its last months), the Coal Merchants' Association levied £100 towards the expenses of a new joint control office to regulate the flow of coal, owing to the scarcity. More happily, the board took the opportunity to congratulate Mr Robert Malcolm Inglis, the Company Secretary who had joined the original Heitons in 1868, on achieving fifty years with the company.[15]

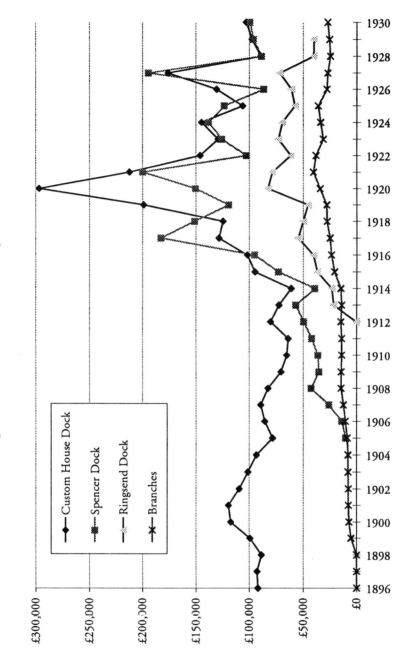

Figure 4.1 *Heitons' Coal Sales by Outlet 1896–1930*

When the war finally came to an end, on 11 November 1918, the firm was faced with a serious situation. Coal was still controlled, and the *St Mirren* was to remain requisitioned by the government for another six months. Over the last few years prices, and with them wages and salaries, had risen alarmingly: the consumer price index had doubled since 1914. In 1912 general wages and salaries were 7 per cent of general costs: by 1920 they were 10 per cent (and in the bad year of 1921, 22 per cent). The three department heads—Leeson, O Giollagain and Maxwell—were now paid between £230 and £270 each, unheard-of salaries a few years before. They were also given a special war bonus of £100. In the same meeting a staff bonus of 20 per cent was approved. In handing out these bonuses, William Hewat underlined the new importance of wages costs, urging that 'in view of the reconstruction work ahead of us, and the burden of the greatly increased wages, the heads of departments should arrange their work so that they shall be as free as possible to devote their time and thought to improving efficiency of working and application of labour saving methods to the greatest possible extent'.[16] W. E. D. Hewat, back from the war in March 1919, was given £250 to act as assistant to the Managing Director. (He was, however, badly gassed in the trenches, and although he joined the board in 1923, he remained a very sick man, never fully recovering his health.)

Politically, events were ominous for a business largely dependent on British trade. The general election in December showed overwhelming support in Ireland (except Ulster) for Sinn Féin, whose policy was largely protectionist. The First Dáil met in the Mansion House on 21 January 1919, and on the same day Dan Breen and others shot a couple of policemen, a crime afterwards glossed as the first act of the War of Independence. De Valera escaped from Lincoln Gaol in February; a general strike broke out in Limerick, and the short-lived Limerick soviet was set up. None of these activities can have made Hewat and the other board members look on the future with a glad eye.

Perhaps it was because of this that when the opportunity arose to buy

Tedcastle McCormick's coal interests, the Managing Director reported that 'he had declined to entertain the price put forward, as being much in excess of what he would be prepared to pay'. This merger would have made the combined firm dominant in the Dublin coal trade. Without knowing the price suggested, it is impossible to say whether this was a good or bad decision. On the other hand, one is tempted to suspect that exhaustion after the events of 1913, the anxieties of the war and the uncertainties of the future led him to turn down a significant opportunity.

Chapter 5
Wars and Rumours of Wars
1920–1939

FOUR YEARS OF WAR left the European nations shaken, tremulous, and fearful of the future. Although the British Empire had finally emerged victorious, the effort had been extreme, and the self-confident power it had enjoyed in Victorian times was gone for ever. Thousands of Irish soldiers (whose very existence the Free State hardly acknowledged) returned to the farms and the towns, often contributing their hard-won military skills to the emerging struggle for freedom. To add to the world's troubles, in 1919 a vicious strain of influenza erupted across the exhausted continents, killing in the end more people than had died in the trenches.

Reporting to the shareholders in September 1919, the firm's Chairman and Managing Director, William Hewat, noted firstly

> the outstanding event of the past year, besides which all else pales into insignificance, namely the successful termination of the great War which strained for so long the energies and resources of the Empire. The management and staff have gladly welcomed back those who have returned from active service, and the Shareholders will join with the Board in mourning for those who have fallen in the fight.

Those reading his words would have well known how badly his eldest son had been gassed in the trenches. Pardonably, William Hewat saw the postwar years simply as a return to straightforward, unregulated trading. The enormous political changes that were about to affect every Irish person were hardly a shadow on the firm's horizon.

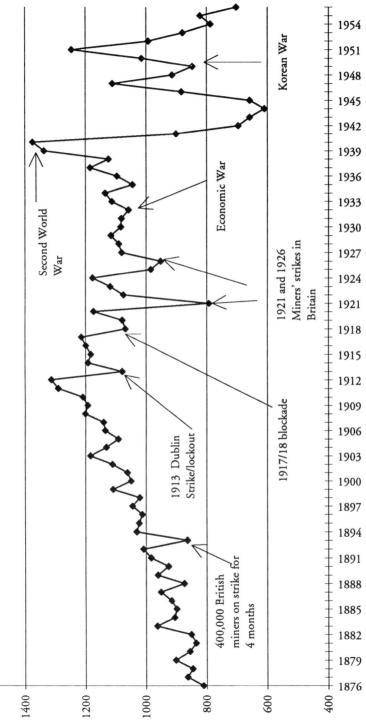

Figure 5.1 *Coal Imported into Dublin 1876–1956*
(Source: *Thom's Directories*)

'While looking forward with confidence,' he continued,

> to the future, it must be recognised that adjustments and altered con-
> ditions have to be faced which will cause dislocation of trade, and the
> need of cooperation is very evident. It is hoped, however, that these
> difficulties may prove temporary, and that with the passing of the war
> clouds a brighter and better future may be in store for the country.

Turning to the detail, Hewat commented that

> during the war repairs and overhauls to the Company's steamers had
> to be deferred and have now to be undertaken, notwithstanding the
> greatly increased cost of the work. The *St Mirren* was reconditioned
> and is again employed in the coal trade, while the *St Margaret*, now
> laid up for repairs, will shortly resume work. Further the Directors
> have availed themselves of an opportunity to build a vessel to replace
> the steamer sunk, and have placed an order with a shipbuilding firm.
> The work of construction is proceeding satisfactorily and it is hoped
> that the new vessel will be ready to take her place as a coal-carrier,
> early in the new year. A new steam crane ordered before the War has
> recently been delivered and forms a valuable addition to the plant
> engaged in the coal trade, while the purchase of three new motor
> lorries improves the position of the Company in the transport branch
> of the business.

As it happened. not long after this was written, the *St Margaret*,
back in service, foundered off Hook Point, carrying coal on a voyage from Troon to Waterford. All of her crew—twelve men—were
lost. A week or so later the newspapers reported that a Mr J. J. Ennis
of Rosslare had discovered a bottle on the strand containing a poign-
ant message scrawled on a cigarette packet:

> St. Margaret, sinking off Hook. Good-bye for ever, my dear friends
> and relations. I will see you no more on earth. Signed Sinclair.'

This however was in the future. Hewat continued:

> It is the intention of the Directors to move the Head Office of the
> Company to George's Quay, and work is proceeding on the new office
> there. This, by relieving the congestion at Westmoreland Street, will
> facilitate the carrying on there of the ordinary departmental and ad-

ministrative work of the Company . . . That there will be a shortage of coal to meet the needs of the country during the winter months seems inevitable, and it is to be hoped that the miners may be induced to put increasing energy into production, so as to avoid (with the help of economy on the part of consumers) an actual scarcity and consequent unemployment.

In fact supplies were to be difficult for the next few years, as the British miners and transport workers engaged on a period of industrial strife. The long period of steady growth in the imports of coal into Dublin that had lasted from the beginning of the Hewat/Inglis partnership in 1877 until 1913 was now definitively over (see graph p. 71). A series of strikes in the 1920s and the Economic War in the 1930s meant that the regular growth of supply was never to be resumed. In March 1921 the tight controls of the wartime years were abolished, and the mines were returned to the owners, a group described by one contemporary authority as 'notable even among postwar British capitalists for their inert stupidity'.[1] Industrial relations immediately deteriorated.

Others besides those in the trade had noticed the likely scarcity, for while the shareholders were considering Hewat's message, the Irish Coal Committee was exploring the possibility of expanding the output of Irish mined coal. The committee discovered that national energy usage at the time was some 4.5 million tons of coal and 5 to 6

Table 5.1: *Estimated Coal Usage in 1919 (all Ireland)*

	Tons (000s)	%
Industrial	1,400	31
Electrical works	125	3
Gas	400	9
Railways	460	10
Domestic	2,115	47
Total	4,500	100

Source: Estimates by Mr T. J. Kettle, Adviser to the Irish Coal Controller at the Irish Coal Committee 1919

million tons of peat (equivalent to 2.5m tons of coal). Local production of coal was running at between 90 and 100,000 tons a year, of which two-thirds came from Castlecomer. 'Local production reached high water mark in 1850, being then 150,000 tons. From that time, when railway facilities enabled the British to compete on more favourable terms in the Irish market, Irish production fell'.[2] The industry employed less than a thousand people in 1919. According to the estimates provided to the committee, the 92,000 tons of Irish coal mined in 1919 constituted a mere 2 per cent of national usage. It was not even enough to meet the needs of the infant electrical industry (see Table 5.1). Although the committee's geological advisers believed that national coal resources amounted to as much as 40 million tons, coal was clearly going to be imported for the foreseeable future.

Although Heitons sold substantial amounts of coal to large industrial customers such as Guinness, to the Tramway Company and gas and electricity plants, the domestic market was crucial. It was estimated that two-thirds of usage in the southern part of the country was for domestic purposes. For this reason, the development of branches in Kingstown/Dún Laoghaire (1898), in Bray (1904) and in Newbridge (1913) was important. (Despite the official change of name after the founding of the new state, the Kingstown branch was so named in the company's ledgers until the 1940s.) At the same time, physical arrangements to allow direct rail connections to the country were established. Following a dispute with the Port and Docks Board over rental for the wharf accommodation at Custom House Dock before the war, the company had established facilities first at Spencer Dock (1904) and then at the Grand Canal Dock, Ringsend (1911).

Heitons may have been cautious in developing its commercial interests, as we have seen in the rejection of the offer to take over Tedcastle McCormick's coal interests, but technologically it was often ahead of the industry. This was evidenced at various levels. As early as 1906 the offices had telephones and were lit by electric light. The technical equipment in the facilities developed before the war was also advanced. The

Spencer Dock wharf was fully equipped with a modern screening plant, a rail siding and steam cranes. This enabled coal to be passed over the screens direct from the ship's hold into railway wagons, thus both saving handling and ensuring coal would be properly screened. Coal was now coming straight out of the mine, and not touching ground again until it reached the ultimate customer's yard. William Hewat had begun exploring the possibilities of using the Dublin United Tramway Company network to move coal as early as 1907, and at Ringsend the company took over and filled in an old graving dock, and tram lines were laid so the Kingstown/Dún Laoghaire branch could be serviced directly. The Ringsend wharf was convenient for south city customers, and also for loading barges for those customers using the Grand Canal. Both of these developments materially aided the development of the country business.

The interwar period started for Heitons with a bumper year. Trading profits in the year ending 31 July 1920 were £51,000 from sales of nearly £600,000 worth (about £24 million in 1995 terms) of coal and iron. Part of this may have been caused by the high prices, which were still under wartime control. In May 1919 the Coal Merchants' Association had presented a petition asking for normal competitive conditions to be resumed, but in fact it wasn't until May 1920 that the board was told 'it is generally expected that decontrol of distribu-

Table 5.2: *Make-up of Trading Profit/(Loss) 1920–40*

Constituent	1920	1925	1930	1935	1940
	%	%	%	%	%
Direct coal sales	67	94	80	65	39
Branches	3	3	4	7	8
Iron & cement	3	2	(1)	9	27
Ships working	19	(10)	2	(8)	19
Other	8	11	15	26	8
Total (£000)	56	25	26	19	45

Source: Heitons' Archive: Private Ledgers 2, 3 and 4

tion will come into operation very soon and Company should prepare for getting back to prewar conditions'. There were also severe coal shortages, particularly in the last months of 1920—it wasn't until 1922 that coal exports from Britain resumed prewar levels.

Over the next twenty years profit contributions from trading (i.e. excluding head office costs and income from rents and dividends) were to average just under £24,000 a year. Head office charges and other overheads amounted to some £15,000 a year, leaving a net profit of £9,000. That average conceals considerable variations, mostly caused by the dramatic political events of the period. For instance, trading profits dipped in 1921/2, following the miners' strike in Britain, and again in the year ending July 1927, reflecting the difficulties caused by the lengthy miners' strike in 1926, which caused British coal output to halve. (It is not clear from the records why the following year was also a bad one for Heitons.) Profits dipped again in 1933, reflecting the beginning of the Economic War, and did not revive until the coal-cattle pacts of 1935 and 1936 came into force.

Since the eighteenth century coal importing had been a competitive, low-margin business. Demand was significantly seasonal, so that capital tied up in ships and dock-side plant was often used at full pitch for the core business only in the winter months. Success required constant attention to the details of operation, squeezing efficiencies out of every process. To enforce this cast of mind, Heitons treated every aspect of the business as a separate profit centre. Every steam crane, every vessel, every branch was expected to make its return, and questions were asked if they did not.

To further the analysis, a notional rent was established for each department—thus in 1915 the new staff committee set the rent for the stables at £150, for the Iron Department in George's Quay at £80, and Head Office, Westmoreland Street, at £180. So that the transport department could have an 'income', notional charges were also set for transport costs—2s 6d per ton for motors to destinations inside the city, 1s 3d per ton for tipping lorries going to Guinness, 1s 6d for lorries going to barracks inside the city, 1s 9d for outside the city. This all required considerable clerical work, and much store was put in Heitons' culture on the keeping of immaculate books.

The annual profit and loss account in the private ledgers shows the contribution made by the three main docks, with Custom House and Spencer Dock contributing similar amounts, and Ringsend slightly less; the contribution of each of the branches was carefully noted, as were those from the Iron and Transport departments. The board used these results for strategic dispositions: thus in 1928 the results from the Newbridge Branch were under consideration, and the minutes noted

> that both the premises and general expenses were too heavy for amount of trade to be done in this district under present conditions. It was decided to carry on during coming months but have clearly in view that any opportunity that may arise for disposing of the premises will be considered. Steps are to be taken to make it known that the property as a whole will be sold to any buyer willing to pay reasonable price for same.

In the event, the branch was not sold at this time.

In an attempt to explore still further the profitability of the various sectors of the company, in September 1934 the board minutes reported:

> it is proposed to segregate Departments as far as possible shewing Capital a/c as well as Profit and Loss Account for each as follows:
>
> Coal Account together with Branches
> Iron Accounts
> Steamers Accounts
> Transport Departments a/cs.
>
> When these are available, the Chairman would desire to have separate board meetings for each, with Head of Department in attendance.[5]

This attempt to identify return on capital employed by department was very advanced for its day. It was, for instance, only in 1933 that the landmark Dunlop group accounts, generally recognised as the first

British consolidated balance sheet and profit and loss accounts, were published. The pioneering experiments in decentralising and control systems in the very biggest US corporations such as General Motors had only taken place in the 1920s.[4]

In addition to his close attention to the business, William Hewat maintained his interest in public affairs. In 1922, just as the Civil War broke out, he was elected President of the Dublin Chamber of Commerce. A year later he was one of five candidates (with his old friend the builder John Good) chosen to represent the Dublin business sector in the general election of August 1923. He stood in Dublin North, then an eight-seater constituency. Also standing for the seat were General Mulcahy, who topped the poll, Alfie Byrne, later to become famous as the long-sitting Lord Mayor of Dublin, Sean T. O'Kelly, later President of Ireland (1945–59), and Ernie O'Malley, the Republican author who began a lengthy hunger strike in prison in October.

In the early years of the new state, many Protestants took no part, regarding its very existence as a betrayal of their caste by English politicians. They were glad to be left alone to behave as far as possible as they had done before the war. Others, like Hewat, took a more positive view. On the hustings he declared he was standing because 'hitherto [businessmen] had been content to take their politics and practically their thoughts from other people—ready-made. This was beneath them. In the formation and foundation of the new order they had got to take their full measure and share of responsibility.'[5] The campaign was not without its problems. The Civil War had only drawn to a halt a few months previously, and the country was full of stories of beatings and reprisals. W. B. Yeats told Lady Gregory that if the Republicans didn't win the election, the government believed that there would be assassinations. Two other business candidates, David Barry and John Good, had meetings broken up by ITGWU activists, and the Businessmen candidates decided to limit their public meetings.

At the polls Hewat gained 2,594 first preference votes, and enough transfers from the dominant Cumann na nGaedheal candidates to clinch a seat after more than twelve counts. No doubt shrewd work by his agent, the solicitor Arthur Cox, contributed to his success. At its next meeting the board decided to 'contribute £300 towards Mr Hewat's expenses, and it was noted with satisfaction that the results of the election placed him in the position of successful candidate'. Not least of the satisfactions must have been the failure of Jim Larkin's close associate P. T. Daly, who was also standing in the constituency, to gain a seat. Larkin himself stood successfully for Dublin North in the second election of 1927, but lost his seat in 1932.

During his four years in the Dáil (he did not stand in the 1927 elections), Hewat bravely and persistently tried to fulfil his mandate of representing Irish business interests. Somewhat to his surprise, he was quickly perceived as the spokesman of the financial and commercial classes. As Professor Magennis of UCD put it: 'in the world of business in the city Deputy Hewat is a species of Pooh Bah; there is hardly any type of enterprise in which he is not active and foremost—one of our chief men in business circles'.[6] Despite this general respect, his interests and the social and political concerns of the bulk of members were far apart. Business was regarded as an important but rather specialised activity, perhaps as the Blood Transfusion Service might be today. The priority given nowadays to financial, industrial and commercial matters simply did not exist. This reflected the structure of the economy. The largest industries were transport, building and clothing which between them employed not much more than 100,000 people. By contrast, there were 128,000 personal domestic servants and 650,000 people working on farms. The common vocabulary of business and economics was still primitive—the very concept of National Income (or GNP) had not yet been worked out.

In a speech on university education, Hewat himself revealed how commercial and industrial activity was perceived as a very special arena, for which a university education was a doubtful asset.

A businessman who sends his sons to college, if he had any intention of their carrying on his business, must run a very grave risk that these boys after they have gone through college would cease to have any intention of going into business. In other words, a training in the University unsuited men in their ideas, not necessarily in their faculties, for commercial pursuits . . . the man who went through college has always been dissatisfied to enter an occupation which his university training made him think was beneath his dignity.[7]

Actually Hewat's practice was not as forthright as his preaching—as he spoke his son Jimmy, who later became Managing Director and Chairman, was preparing to graduate from Trinity, as was his daughter Elspeth, who became a doctor.

Many of the debates in which Hewat took part read as if he and the leader of the Labour Party, Thomas Johnson, were having a private capital versus labour dialogue. His very first intervention, for instance, on 2 September 1923, was to refute a point Johnson had made about wages. Hewat took a robust view of social and interventionist schemes generally. He vigorously opposed the payment of dole money to 'the man who is prepared to put his back to the wall and to stand all day and do nothing'. He opposed schemes of railway amalgamation, because 'during the war it was considered necessary that the Government should take control of the railways and speaking as a commercial man, I do not think the result of that experience has convinced very many traders that they are going to benefit'. He was strongly opposed to price control. His cautious approach to investment and a marked dislike of government intervention in commercial affairs led to his voting against the Shannon Scheme, on the grounds that the project would absorb costs representing 20 per cent of the government's annual income to provide two and a half times more electricity than the country needed.

Over time Hewat became a practised and frequent speaker in the Dáil. In 1925 he successfully piloted a Bill through the Dáil making certain changes to the Port and Docks Board's constitution (naturally, opposed all the way by Johnson). In truth, however, the mentality of the other members was generally far from the commercial common sense he strove to inject. This is hardly surprising, for the times were strenuous and demanding. As William Cosgrave and his Ministers attempted to establish the style and customs of a new state, outside prowled the losers in the Civil War, snarling their contempt for 'little Liam the potboy' and his betrayal of the Republican dream. In October 1923 the several hundred Republicans in prison in Dublin staged a well-publicised hunger strike. The following year the Army Mutiny momentarily exposed the weak foundations of the state, leading to ministerial resignations. While Jim Larkin was in Moscow, joining the Stalin-dominated Third International, members of his Workers' Union of Ireland had to be forcibly ejected from Liberty Hall by the army. In 1926 de Valera founded Fianna Fáil, which was followed by a long series of attacks by the IRA on police barracks, judges and jurymen throughout the country. In 1927 Kevin O'Higgins was assassinated.

The time and the context were clearly not ripe for the kind of bread and butter issues that William Hewat represented. With hindsight, it appears that the Dublin businessmen's sponsorship of TDs had a certain naivety about it. For instance, in a joint advertisement issued during the 1923 election campaign, the five candidates declared: 'when great commercial problems arise in the years of development ahead, we believe that businessmen of long experience should be there to tackle them in a vigorous businesslike manner'.[8] Complex political issues are hardly susceptible to such an approach, nor are party politicians generally grateful for such assistance.

During his time in the Dáil, the firm was presented with an unpleasant reminder of the dreadful days of 1913. In pursuit of his fierce personal battle with the leaders of the ITGWU, Larkin and his Workers' Union of Ireland fomented a strike in the docks in 1925. As usual with Larkin-led strikes, animosity was quickly whipped into violence, with WUI men pelting ITGWU workers with stones and blocks of coal.[9] The Heitons board minutes described the outcome in November 1925:

during the period from 16 July . . . owing to Workers' Union members refusing to take coal from members of the Irish Transport Union a prolonged struggle has been in operation controlled by the [Coal Merchants'] Association as a whole on behalf of its 23 members. Gradually and in spite of every form of intimidation and outrage the Transport Union, working in conjunction with our organisation has succeeded in first discharging the steamers held up for nearly a month in the Port and latterly in connection with deliveries of coal, have apparently broken down the opposition and seem in a fair way to resume normal working at the Yards. Larkin and the Workers' Union at a stage in the dispute commenced importing coal to Dublin and distributing same by means of carts direct from steamers and notwithstanding efforts made by the Association to get shipowners and colliery agents to refuse supplies a large quantity of coal came through in this way. It is not however thought that this has proved a successful venture or profitable for anyone concerned.

At the same meeting as this grimly satisfactory report was made, William Hewat, who was now sixty, relinquished his position as Managing Director of the company, and his son Cecil Hewat became joint Managing Director with Hamilton Whiteside. J. Denham Macalister took over C. D. Hewat's position as Company Secretary.

As we have seen, the General Strike in Britain and its long aftermath hit profits. In 1925, the British coal-owners demanded heavy wage cuts and a lengthening of hours. Since Churchill had put Britain back on the gold standard, thus effectively taxing all exports, wages were threatened in other industries too. In May 1926 the miners went on strike, supported by transport workers, iron and steelmen, chemical workers, building workers and electricity and gas workers supplying industry. In the silent streets politically naive undergraduates played at being tram-drivers. On 6 May the staff committee minutes recorded that 'as there was no coal available [from Britain] . . . it was decided to pay off the crews and lie up the steamers. Crews were paid off as from, Wednesday last, the *St Kenneth* being in Custom House Dock, the *St Fintan* Ringsend, and *St Mungo* Spencer'. By 27 May the General Strike was over, but the miners remained out, and coal exports were restricted. The staff committee notes: 'the shortage of coal is getting increasingly felt—arrangements have been made with Messrs Guinness, Dublin Commissioners, Tramway Coy and SR Railway to import cargo from America and this is being arranged through a firm in London'.

The first steamer from America arrived on 1 July and discharged its 4,500 tons of cargo in the unexpectedly quick time of seven days. It should be remembered that this load was ten times larger than the usual cross-channel cargo, which gave rise to numerous handling problems. Over the next few months numerous other cargoes came from the US, but these stopgap measures were not enough. Throughout the strike Heitons processed less than half the tonnage they would have normally imported. In one dreadful week in early September a mere 374 tons came through the firm's facilities on the three docks, a mere 10 per cent of a typical throughput. In October, with the strike still continuing, the staff committee noted a 'great shortage of coal in Dublin—pressure for deliveries increases with nothing available'. Since Ireland was almost totally dependent for its heat, light and industrial power on imported coal, the government actually contributed £95,208 for the 'purchase and importation of fuel during Coal Emergency'. Heitons ordered 2,000 tons of coal briquettes from Germany, and the firm was participating in the Coal Merchants' Association's joint purchases of coal. Later in the month the firm distributed 250 tons of coal free of charge 'to assist relieving distress among the poor of Dublin'. For those who remembered the bitter days of 1913, there must have been some wry interest in recording that 'the firm have also rendered various services in cartage of turf etc. from the country free of charge for the Transport and General Workers Union'.

The British miners' strike came to an end in late November 1926. Restrictions on coal exports were soon lifted, leaving the firm with a large quantity of expensive American coal on the high seas. It was quickly decided that no British coal would be bought until the US stocks had been sold. In all, twelve large cargoes of coal arrived between the end of the strike and the discharge of the last on 13 January 1927. By this time prices had begun tumbling to more normal levels. When these shipments were ordered, coal was being sold in Dublin at more than 100s a ton; they had to be sold eventually at prices of 30s to 40s, entailing substantial losses.

As a consequence of these difficulties, it was not until 1930 and 1931 that trading profits reached the average level for the interwar years. A persistent problem during the whole of this period was the return on shipping. Apart from the premises, the steam colliers were the company's most significant asset, and they were making continuous losses. In the fifteen years between 1920 and 1935 the Shipping Department recorded profits in only four annual accounts. The board recognised this was not due to bad management, but was a function of the general depression in tramp and coasting trades in Britain and Ireland. Freight rates throughout the 1920s were low, and were to drop further still in the 1930s.[10] In March 1925 the board bleakly noted:

generally the outlook recognised as being unfavourable for any imme-

Table 5.3: *Balance Sheet Structure Year Ending 31 July 1936*

Assets	£	Financed by	£
Premises	82,100	Capital	
Dockside plant	4,900	Preference shares	70,000
Colliers	24,000	Ordinary shares	60,000
Motor lorries etc.	8,500		
Horses etc.	1,300	Creditors	20,000
Stock	32,900		
Debtors	52,100	Reserves	62,400
Investments	17,000	Profit	17,000
Cash	4,100		
Miscellaneous	2,500		
Total	229,400	*Total*	229,400

Source: Heitons' Archive: Private Ledgers

Table 5.4: *Clerical Staff by Length of Service (1946)*

Years of service	No.	% of staff
0–5	22	28
6–10	11	14
11–15	18	23
16–20	8	10
21–30	13	17
31–40	3	4
40+	3	4
Total	78	100

Source: Heitons' Archive: workings by J. Denham Macalister

diate improvement in freights . . . *St Mirren*: it was decided to let her lie in the meantime. There is still a month's work on repairs. *St Mungo* and *St Fintan*: Dublin to keep these boats going. *St Kenneth*: when clear of Limerick cargo, Mr Harper will endeavour to get freights to keep her going on outside work for a week or so, but we must face tying her up if results do not warrant her continuing to run outside of Dublin coal business, which cannot provide cargoes for her.

After some years of dissatisfaction, in 1933 management of the fleet was shifted from Glasgow to Dublin. The arrangement had been set up when the firm first invested in steam vessels, and when Glasgow was at the height of its prosperity as a centre of shipping. The close relationship with Harpers, who also ran their own ships and acted as coal agents for several mineowners, was maintained, with Hugh Harper remaining on the board. However, as the world depression deepened, and the implications of the Economic War between Britain and Ireland took hold, the old arrangement made less sense. A qualified marine engineer, Mr W. E. G. Wallace, a large, ebullient Scot, was recruited from Harpers to handle the fleet from Dublin with the title of Marine Superintendent. The importance of his position was quickly recognised by his rapid elevation to the new board of management which replaced the old staff committee in 1931. Wallace moved to Glasnevin from Glasgow, and remained with the firm until his death in July 1955.

An important feature of the post-First World War period was the gradual realisation by employers that it was desirable and necessary to plan for their employees' lives in retirement. In the past the expectation had been that workers would either make their own arrangements, or work until they died. As health conditions changed, Heitons and other long-lived firms were increasingly faced with the problem of respected employees who were simply too old and frail to continue, and yet had no other means of support. Heitons' staff, who were often recruited as youngsters. frequently achieved remarkable lengths of service with the firm. In 1946 the then Secretary, J. Denham Macalister, noted that the average length of service of the 78 clerical workers was fifteen years. Fully a quarter of the staff had twenty years service or more (see Table 5.4)—that is to say they would remember the impact of the British General Strike of 1926 had on the firm. Six of the staff had joined the firm before the First World War. This was not simply a passing phase—one of the young men who joined the firm in 1945 was Sid Kane, who eventually retired as Company Secretary 43 years later, in 1988. As time went on, men and women came into the firm whose parents had served, and in some cases were still serving, generating an almost 'family' atmosphere. The benefits of such loyal staff have always been particularly fostered and appreciated by the directors.

Throughout the 1920s men and women coming to retirement were given ex gratia payments by the board. In 1931 it was decided to put the whole thing on a proper footing, and a contributory pension scheme was established for clerical staff with the Sun Life Insurance Co. The social responsibility implied in establishing a proper scheme of this sort can hardly be exaggerated. Many of Hewat's business colleagues failed to do so. When insolvency hit so many old Irish companies in the newly competitive conditions of the 1960s and 1970s, they had unfunded pension schemes, and employees with twenty or thirty years service were left with nothing.[11]

The general election of 1932 initiated a crucial change in the management of the Irish economy. De Valera's Fianna Fáil party, supported by the Labour Party, mustered enough votes to form a government and at once set about putting its policies into action. First an increasingly elaborate network of tariffs was established, and then, in June 1932, the payment due on the Land Annuities was refused.

These payments arose under the Land Acts (1880–1912), under which Irish landlords were bought out by the government, and the land sold to small farmers at long purchase rates. When the new state was established, the annuities formed part of the complicated Ultimate Financial Settlement between the Irish and British governments. Fianna Fail, however, did not feel itself bound by the decisions of the previous government, taking the view that it was against natural justice to make the Irish people pay for land that should have been theirs anyway. The opposition parties felt that these issues had been thoroughly thrashed out in long and difficult negotiations between 1923 and 1926, and deplored the irresponsibility of reneging on national obligations. Although the annuities had been a key issue in the election, there had been little discussion of what Britain's reaction might be to the abrupt cutting off of this income in the depression days of the early 1930s. The fact that Ireland was simultaneously netting some £3.5 million a year from Britain through the illegal selling of tickets in the Hospital Sweepstakes merely added insult to injury.

Payment of the annuities was withheld in June 1932, and by mid-July a 20 per cent duty had been imposed on the bulk of Irish exports to Britain, the destination of over 90 per cent of them. The Irish government retaliated with a similar duty on British exports to Ireland. The Fianna Fáil government was again 'at war' with the old enemy—Frank Aiken and Seán MacEntee made rousing speeches declaring how much better off the country would be now that Irish food and other goods were to be consumed by the Irish, not the British. Among the first commodities to be hit by duties and then by supply quotas was coal. With the experience of 1926 behind it, however, the Dublin coal trade began to look for supplies from elsewhere.

Within a year or so coal was being shipped into Dublin from Belgium and the United States, and the coal-owners of South Wales began to complain to the British government about the loss of their market. In January 1935 the first coal-cattle pact between the two countries was announced. The British government increased the quota of Irish cattle allowed to enter the UK, greatly easing pressure on the Irish farming sector. In exchange the Irish government allowed the purchase of an equivalent value of British coal, ensuring that virtually all coal imported into Ireland came from British mines. The special duties on both cattle and coal remained, however, until the final trade agreement in 1938.

A few months after the first coal-cattle pact was signed, the firm's Chairman, William Hewat, died on 15 May 1935, in his seventieth year. During his long association with the firm he had consolidated its position as one of the leading merchant houses in the city, a position it retained through extremely testing times. Despite very tight control of the business—even after his death staff referred to him as 'the Guvnor'—he filled many roles in Dublin life, being one of the important few who persuaded the ordinary Protestant business community to take part in the new state. For this he was very well qualified, having in his time worked closely with William Martin Murphy, the leader of the previous generation, and having acted himself as TD, as Chairman of Dublin Port and Docks Board, as President of the Dublin Chamber of Commerce, as a leading member of the Coal Merchants' Association, as a long-serving director and latterly Chairman of the Dublin United Tramway Company, and of the Commercial Insurance Company.

A few years before his death he had handed over the managing directorship of the firm to his son Cecil Hewat. He had fought in the First World War, and had come into the business after that. Before becoming Managing Director he had been Company Secretary. He is remembered especially as a man with high professional and technical standards, but also one who took trouble to get to know the staff and even the regular casual dockers very well.

In his first full year in charge of the business, Heitons sold 200,000 tons of coal, receiving £1.56 per ton. This was in fact a ten-year peak, no doubt related to the political situation. The country as a whole was importing some 2.5 million tons, giving the firm an 8 per cent market share overall, although its importance in the domestic market would have been higher. Financially and operationally the firm was in a strong position. Its shares were held by a tight group, mostly consisting of family members, and it had no other major liabilities. The bank overdraft of £3,382 was well covered by the deposit account of £5,000. The ratio of debtors to creditors (2.6:1) was healthy, and the record sales gave rise to a profit after a head office overhead of £17,000, allowing for a 7 per cent dividend on the ordinary shares.

From a wider perspective, however, it was possible to perceive clouds on the horizon. The Fianna Fáil government had embarked on the Economic War during a world depression without much heed to the economic consequences; although the coal-cattle pacts had been established, there was as yet no sign of a further thaw. Furthermore, it was clear that the government was pursuing a policy of positive discrimination in favour of Catholic firms, and local sources of energy as far as possible.

The international situation, with the coming to power of Hitler in 1933, the Spanish Civil War and the Japanese invasion of Manchuria, was full of foreboding. Whatever else happened in the world, Britain and Germany would hardly be able to remain aloof, which in turn meant the likelihood of severe problems with coal supply. The vulnerability of merchant shipping, so clearly demonstrated at the end of the previous war, when the *St Mungo* and hundreds of other vessels had been sunk, was a vivid memory.

This somewhat gloomy outlook was improved in 1938 by the new trade agreement between Britain and Ireland, but only as the international situation worsened. By 1939 most people had begun to lose hope of averting war; by 2 September, after Hitler invaded Poland, a new world war became inevitable, and de Valera declared Ireland's intention of remaining neutral. The 'Emergency' began, a Department of Supplies was set up, and the country and the firm braced themselves for a long and difficult period in which coal, and fuel generally, would be in very short supply.

Chapter 6
In Plato's Cave 1939–1957

F ROM THE OUTBREAK OF WAR in 1939 Ireland began a twenty-year period of isolation from the harsh events of the busy world. Partly through accidents of world history, partly through choice, the country lived during the war years, as the Trinity historian F. S. L. Lyons put it, 'in Plato's cave, backs to the fire of life, and deriving their only knowledge of what went on outside from the flickering shadows thrown on the wall before their eyes by the men and women who passed to and from behind them'.

Even after the war, the country, with its deeply agricultural society, its dim and protected business sector and its profound Catholicism, stayed largely remote from the intellectual and economic currents of the day. For some this was less a deprivation than a deliberate policy to preserve Ireland as 'the home of a people who valued material wealth only as the basis of right living, of a people who were satisfied with frugal comfort and devoted their leisure to the things of the spirit', as de Valera famously put it. He was by no means alone in this aspiration. John Ryan, the writer and editor, saw that during the war 'the simple goodness of things was emphasised rather than diminished by the absence of superfluous luxuries. The country was clean, uncluttered and unhurried. There was no tourism. We could not travel abroad nor could the world come to view us.'[1]

For all sorts of practical and symbolic reasons, neutrality was the least unsatisfactory policy de Valera could endorse. Entering the war on the Axis side, as urged by Republican extremists, would have been strategically ill advised, if nothing worse. Anti-British feeling was still strong, and there was reason to fear that an alliance with Britain may have provoked another civil war, perhaps financed by Germany. During the Battle of the Atlantic in the early years of the war, Ireland's neutrality, and the consequent refusal to allow the British Navy to re-occupy the Treaty Ports, engendered great bitterness in England, and uneasiness among the more pro-British Irish people. The novelist Nicholas Monsarrat, who had been at sea himself in the Atlantic, sourly recreated how the sailors escorting the convoys felt: 'the bases were denied . . . the cost in men and ships added months to the struggle, and ran a score which Irish eyes a-smiling on the day of Allied victory were not going to cancel . . . they sailed past this smug coastline, past

Table 6.1: *Planning Energy Usage During the Emergency**

Essential users	*(000 tons pa)*	
Anthracite	45	
Domestic	450	
Railways	230	
Gas	400	
Industry (inc. ESB)	600	
Total		1,700
Less available home resources		
Extra turf (tons coal equivalent)	250	
Home coal	120	
Wood (tons coal equivalent)	50	
Coke	100	
Total		520

Leaving a minumum import requirement of: 1,205

*The figures do not add up: The Department was clearly working with estimates and round figures.

Source: PRO Dept. of Taoiseach S 11944A

people who did not give a damn how the war went as long as they could live on in their fairy-tale world'.[2]

It is unlikely that Heitons' chairman, Cecil Hewat, or his brother Willie, who had fought in the British Army in the First World War, would have expressed themselves so bitterly, especially since they would have been extremely conscious of the serious risks that their own crews were running in bringing essential goods across the Irish Sea. The fates of the *St Mungo* in 1917 and the *St Fintan* in 1941, with the deaths of twenty-one men, showed how real the risks were. It is, however, equally unlikely that they felt that the country's policy did it any credit. In practice, there was a great deal of covert cooperation between Ireland and Britain that junior naval officers would have been quite unaware of. Ireland's secret policy was to provide so much value that Britain would lose more by, for instance, seizing the Treaty Ports, than she would gain by cooperation.

The war situation, however, created very serious supply problems. Even before war broke out prudent users, such as the gas company, the sugar company and the Great Southern Railway, were building up stocks of coal. In 1939 and 1940, during the phoney war period, the record quantity of 2.7m tons of coal was shipped into Dublin. This was a hundred thousand tons more than the previous two-year record, in 1911 and 1912, and a record that was never to be beaten.

There was obviously something of a race against time to get in as much coal as possible. In July 1939 Heitons alone imported 21,000 tons in 36 boats. These cargoes came from eleven different British ports, including Ayr, Glasgow, Whitehaven, Workington, Manchester (via the Ship Canal), Troon, Cardiff and Swansea. Most of these were between 200 and 400 tons, although there were three larger cargoes of just less than 2,000 tons, two of which went straight to Cork, and one was discharged at North Wall. On the second working day of the Emergency, 5 September, panic buyers forced the coal offices to close their doors at 1 pm.[3] Similar rush buying of threatened materials led to unprecedented profits in 1939/40 and 1940/1 in the Iron

Department.

The outbreak of war and the declaration of neutrality had effectively shut Ireland off from key supplies. Iron, steel, petrol, tea, sugar, tobacco, wheat for bread and most of all coal were all going to be in increasingly short supply. A memo to the Taoiseach's department reckoned that the peacetime usage for the country as a whole were 2.5 million tons, of which 1.5 million were for domestic use. The biggest squeeze would naturally occur in this sector. Although the protectionist policies of the 1930s had enabled an industrial sector of sorts to evolve, fuel and its concomitant, power, were not to be conjured out of the air. The country was completely dependent on the 2.5 million tons of coal imported from Britain every year. So when the British cut exports of coal from 40 million tons to a mere 5 million tons in 1941, Ireland was bound to suffer.

A year later, in July 1940, during the 'phoney war', Heitons imported 23,000 tons in a single month. It came in on 47 separate cargoes, a record that was never to be beaten. The physical work involved in discharging one of these cargoes makes this an impressive feat. In essence the task was not much changed since it had been described thirty years in *The History of a Black Diamond*. As the vessel pulled in to the quay, the firm's ship's agent went on board, and sorted out the various papers. Then the diggers clambered into the hold clutching their great shovels. Their job was to shovel the coal into one of four large metal tubs which were then picked up by the steam crane and swung ashore. In the hot dusty hold there were four men to a tub, digging coal for all they were worth (being paid by the ton). The great crane picked up the first tub and swung it out of the hold over an existing heap of coal (containing perhaps 500 tons), where a 'canter', pushed down a lever on the side of the tub and let the coal out. This could be a dangerous job, as the tubs containing one and a half tons of coal were suspended from a height, and often swung erratically (particularly in the wind), and a man could very easily be knocked off.

Once the tub was empty, the craneman then swung it almost in one smooth movement, back into the hold, guided always by the 'singer-out'—for high up in the crane's cabin the craneman could not see into the hold. The lives of the sixteen men, digging for dear life in the dust and stench of the hold, hardly looking up, depended on the 'singer-out' to prevent the craneman from dropping the heavy tubs on top of them.

Although dock work was casual, many men preferred to work regularly for one particular merchant such as Heitons. (It was not until 1961 that mechanised grabs were used to lift the coal out of ships' holds.) So skilled and quick did the regular teams become that the crane with full and empty tubs seemed to be in almost continuous movement, going much faster than similar cranes do now on building sites. A Heitons' clerk recorded the type and destination of every consignment as it pulled out. (If the coal was being brought into Ocean Pier or the river, this job, standing unprotected for as much as twelve hours in the cold of the quayside, was one of the least popular office chores.) Five cargoes in a day meant that the men shifted some 1,500 tons between them.

In June 1940 coal rationing was introduced, limiting each household to half a ton a month. In 1941 the board was presented with a clear reminder of just how dangerous the Irish Sea could be to merchant shipping. In March the *St Fintan* was sunk with all hands on the way to Cardiff to collect a cargo of coal. As the historian of the Irish merchant marine during the war put it:

> At 4 pm on 22 March 1941 when off the Pembrokeshire coast she was attacked by two German bombers and sunk with her crew of nine. There were no survivors. The scene was witnessed by a Milford Haven trawler which steamed through the wreckage and picked up one body, that of Chief Engineer Howat. The cook, L. McGuinness, survived because he had not sailed on the *St Fintan*. He had travelled from Drogheda to his home in Ringsend, Dublin, for the day as the ship lay in the Boyne and had missed the train back.[4]

This was, of course, the second of Heitons' ships to be sunk by the Germans. The minutes of the same board meeting (30 September

1941) recorded a touch of revenge. The *St Eunan*, which as a British registered vessel carried a small gun on the poop deck and a naval gunner, had 'received extensive damage as a result of a mine explosion while on a passage from Cardiff to Dublin on 6 May 1941'. But 'the same vessel was attacked from the air in the same waters on the morning of 25 September 1941 when the plane is believed to have been destroyed by *St Eunan's* fire'. The Marine Superintendent, W. E. G. Wallace, was authorised to arrange for the purchase of suitable memento gifts for the officers and crew.

In January 1941, in the face of continuing losses, shipping to Irish ports was restricted, and rationing of a range of basic goods such as tea and wheat flour became inevitable. Coal was already rationed to half a ton per month per household. Six months later this was reduced to a quarter of a ton for the months between March and October. Later it became virtually impossible for domestic consumers to buy coal at all. Most of it was now allocated to large industrial customers. In September 1941, for instance, the firm imported coal specifically and by licence for Guinness, the Great Southern Railway, the ESB, Irish Oil and Cake, Jameson, the Swastika Laundry, Dublin Port and Docks and Minch Norton, the maltsters.

In 1941 coal imports to Dublin fell to a level last seen sixty years before; the following year they were to drop a further 30 per cent. Over the next four years the annual discharge of coal into Dublin was 40 per cent less than the average annual intake in the 1930s. The comparison is, furthermore, misleading since the Department of Supplies routed most Irish coal through Dublin, at the expense of ports such as Cork and Waterford. Coal import licences were handed out on a quota basis by the Department of Supplies. The quota was based on the previous year's importation, and, with a view to increasing Heitons' quota, the firm bought the old-established coal importer of J. J. Carroll in 1944. This firm had been started as a sideline by the owner of the Brazen Head in Bridge Street in 1830, and had been run by the Carroll family ever since. By 1883 James J. Carroll, the son, owned eight sailing vessels and a steamship specially built for Spencer Dock, where he had a depot for the despatch of coal in railway wagons to all parts of the country. The chairman of Carrolls, V. Arnold Carroll, became a member of Heitons' board, and later (in 1949) a Director of the Bank of Ireland.

Such was the scramble for coal that the larger users were sometimes tempted to apply for import licences themselves. Later in the war the Coal Merchants' Association made furious representations to the Department of Supplies complaining that end-users rather than established coal importers had been granted import licences. Certainly the officials at the English end must have been more than a little surprised to see a licence authorising the Swastika Laundry (one of those specifically complained of) to import coal!

The lack of coal did not reduce the ordinary citizen's desire for hot food, warm water and protection against the chill of winter. Other fuels had therefore to be provided. For the next six years, until supplies of coal resumed in 1948, as much as half of Heitons' business was in 'locals', mostly turf, wood and coke. Heitons' first cargo of pitch arrived in September 1941. One of the uses of pitch was to create 'duff', a deeply unsatisfactory mixture of coal dust and pitch much used by the Great Southern Railway. This was so dirty a fuel that the crew had regularly to clean out the fire, sometimes after travelling only a few miles. As a result train journeys took a long time— the Dublin to Athlone trains were regularly overtaken by the canal boats. On the other hand there was often no alternative method of travel, petrol being even more tightly controlled than coal.

The accounts for the winter of 1940/1 show a huge increase in the sales of turf; the firm bought a couple of bogs near Monasterevin— incidentally making losses on both—and a wood. By the winter of 1942/3 the yards were stacked high with turf, and the firm was selling over 5,000 tons a month. Mountains of turf appeared in the Phoenix Park, and camps of volunteers and soldiers were set up in bogs all over the country to save turf. A year later the firm was actually selling a

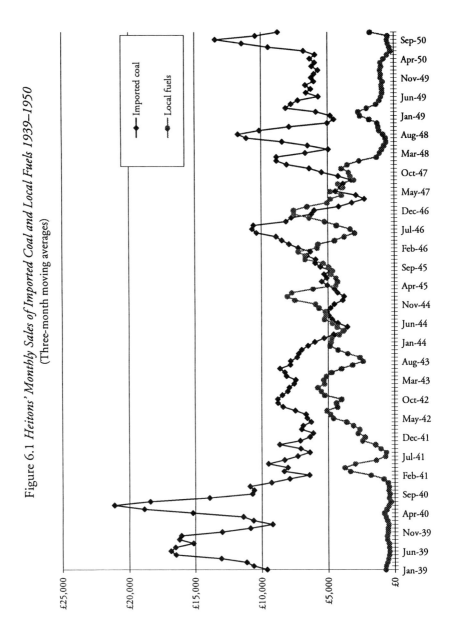

Figure 6.1 *Heitons' Monthly Sales of Imported Coal and Local Fuels 1939–1950*
(Three-month moving averages)

greater tonnage of turf than coal. It was not until the winter of 1947/ 8 that coal re-established its position as the predominant product, and even then there were regular winter peaks of turf sales, and at times of difficulty such as the Korean War (1950–3).

In 1941 the firm made another attempt to meet the insatiable demand for fuel products, this time by marketing a patent fuel, under the mildly unfortunate brand name of Heitoids. This consisted of balls of coal slack, with tiny amounts of turf and coal screenings for good measure, held together with pitch. The ratio in the finished product was 75 per cent slack to 25 per cent pitch. It was made by a machine specially imported from Leeds.[5] In the first year nearly 7,000 tons were sold at £3 12s 7d each, returning a profit of £1,128 on a capital investment of £6,250. The following year 8,900 tons were sold, and in 1944 sales of 8,800 tons produced a trading profit of £2,966. Encouraged by this success, the firm bought a second plant, which produced a better-quality product. The new plant mixed coke and breeze with pitch in the ratio of nearly 90:1. Although this product was priced originally at £4 a ton and then at £4 10s, this plant never made a profit, and when it was closed in 1948 it had a cumulated deficit of £3,899. Even the No. 1 plant, selling a much lower-quality product, began to make losses, so that when it was closed down in 1949 the total of 44,000 tons sold over eight years had made the miserable net contribution of £335.

The war was a period of make-do and mend, an uncertain time of improvisation in which it was hardly appropriate or even possible to make long-term plans. This difficulty was particularly felt in respect to the fleet. The Shipping Department had always been central to the firm's activity, and the pivot of its profitability. The years when the ships made money were good years for the firm as a whole. After the sinking of the *St Fintan* (which was insured for £14,450), the board considered the building of a replacement, but deferred making a decision. In 1944, with the fleet consisting of the *St Mungo*, the *St Kenneth* and the *St Eunan*, they came back to the question. As the minutes of

the meeting of 4 October (four months after D-Day, with the Allied
Armies at the German border, between Trier and Aachen) record:

> a general discussion took place on postwar policy and future plans for the
> various departments with special reference to future of shipping. Owing
> to uncertainty of the time and lack of information available no final
> decisions could be come to but it was generally agreed that as soon as the
> time was judged to be propitious the *St Kenneth* should be replaced by a
> 1,200 tons deadweight Custom House Dock boat and that at the same
> time the building of a second such vessel should be seriously considered,
> the directors meantime to watch developments very closely . . . the pros-
> pects of new lines for the Iron Department and Engineering section were
> also discussed.

The *St Kenneth*, which was eventually sold in 1953, had a deadweight
tonnage of about 850 tons and a summer carrying capacity of 750
tons. In the event nothing was done until the second *St Fintan* was
added to the fleet in 1947. This was a small and elderly vessel, originally built in 1904, of only 368 gross tonnage (for full details see
Appendix 2).

The victory of the Allies in 1945 left Europe's economy in a desperate state, and it wasn't until the Marshall Plan got going in 1947 that
the way forward could be clearly seen. American aid and effort were
primarily devoted to rehabilitating the shattered and starving peoples
of Western Europe such as France, Italy, the Netherlands and Germany. Ireland, whose neutral stance had at times irritated the Ameri-
cans as much as the British, was not high on anyone's agenda. The
country was still predominantly agricultural, with Britain as the main
market. Since Britain was itself one of the slowest growing countries,
which protected its farmers by subsidising a cheap food policy, this
was not a position of strength. The Irish business sector was still heavily protected by the Control of Manufactures Acts 1932–4, which,
among other regulations, restricted foreign nationals from owning
companies in Ireland. As a result the Irish business elite, a small group
of some one hundred families, dominated the large companies with
interlocking shareholdings. When the fierce winds of serious economic
competition hit this complacent group in the 1960s and 1970s, few

survived. Those that did, such as Heitons, had special qualities.

Coal supplies remained difficult for most of the 1940s, and any source of fuel was accepted. In June 1947, for instance, the firm discharged twelve cargoes in all, with a miscellany of fuel products including American coal from Baltimore, fossil wood from Antwerp, anthracite duff from Swansea, slurry (wet slack) from Silloth and lignite from Teignmouth. None of these products were anything like the quality that had been imported before the war. (US coal, incidentally, came under the strict condition that it was not to be re-exported to any Soviet country.) So great was the hunger for any coal at all that even small amounts were valuable. In 1946 the German ship *Travemunde* ran short of bunker coal and put into Dublin. Twenty tons of coal was supplied by Dohertys under instruction from the Department of Supplies. Towards the end of the year the *Travemunde* returned the coal to Dublin. Although the coal was legally the Department's, Dohertys certainly expected they would be allowed to discharge and sell it. However Heitons heard of the arrival first, and quickly offered to help the Department to discharge the coal. This was accepted. By the time Dohertys heard of the matter, the coal was discharged, and, despite threats of legal action, there the matter rested.

By 1948 however more normal conditions were returning. British household coal was coming back into the market—in November 1948, for instance, the firm discharged fifteen cargoes of coal, ten of which were household coal. This improvement was briefly interrupted in

Table 6.2: *Contribution to Trading Profit (%)*

	1945	1950	1955	1960
Fuels	29	18	29	38
Iron Department	27	67	39	39
Branches	0	9	7	13
Shipping	27	(1)	11	–
Total (£000)	42	69	61	91

Source: Heitons' Archive: Private Ledgers

1950 and 1951 during the Korean War when once again raw material prices became prohibitive. For another year Heitons went back to turf, before a steady increase in the tonnage of coal sold by the firm, which lasted from 1951 to 1955, gave a promise of a return to normality. Another war, this time the Suez Crisis, broke that dream, and the long downward slide in industrial and domestic use of coal began.

At the same time the historical trend to larger cargoes was resumed. At the beginning of the nineteenth century cargoes of 50 tons were the rule; at the beginning of the twentieth 200–300 tons were typical; in 1948 cargoes of 3,800 tons and more began to appear in the cargo books, five times the typical size of the cargoes shipped by Heitons' own fleet. This trend was to continue throughout the 1950s, until by 1959 the *Senator Possehl* from the US was shipping 12,000 tons or more in a single cargo.

These large ships from relatively exotic ports added a touch of variety to the work of the firm. As Sid Kane, then ship's agent and later Company Secretary, remembers, the crews could bring both life and death with them. Since the firm was responsible for preventing crew members from illegally staying in the country, long days were spent searching for the pregnant stewardess of the *Havgast,* who had discharged herself from Sir Patrick Dun's hospital before hiding out in the South Circular Road area. Less time was wasted by the Finnish Radio Officer who had died at sea, or his compatriot who went missing just before his ship sailed. His body washed up in the Liffey a week later. Both were buried in Mount Jerome. A more typical adventure was that of the German second officer who was arrested after drunkenly disputing a taxi fare. The officer, who had been in submarines during the war, so impressed the district justice by his bowing and heel clicking, his accurate English, his frequent 'my lord' and his immaculate uniform, that the case was dismissed. This did not prevent his captain, whose war career by contrast passed on a Baltic ferry, from seizing the opportunity to send the officer home. Occasionally a seamy side to Dublin life was revealed, as when a long-missing sea-

Table 6.3: *The Iron Department Takes Off (1950 & 1960)*

Section		1950 Sales (£000)	1950 Gross Profit (%)	1960 Sales (£000)	1960 Gross Profit (%)
A	Welding	21.4	14.9	36.5	13.2
B	Bars (metals)	216.9	16.0	571.8	13.3
C	Cement	86.7	1.6	95.1	6.9
E	Engineering	17.9	11.7	43.4	18.6
H	Hardware	61.9	6.8	103.3	17.3
P	Plumbing	–	–	18.8	16.7
Total		404.8	11.2	868.9	13.4

Source: Heitons' Archive: Private Ledgers

man was discovered in north Dublin comfortably tucked up in bed with both a mother and her daughter. Not long after the Cuban Missile crisis, Russian ships started to bring coal. In those hyper-sensitive days at the height of the Cold War, the international implications of a defection added an extra dimension to the firm's responsibility to the Aliens Office. In fact no Russian seamen attempted to defect, not even those who had to spend days or weeks in hospital after some accident on board. Perhaps the watchful attentions of the local *Pravda* correspondent, reputed to have been a KGB major, had something to do with this.

Twelve thousand tons were more than any one merchant could handle at once, so these cargoes would be shared. Also in 1950, during the Korean crisis, Polish coal began to appear in the cargo books. The first shipment was of 3,000 tons from Gdansk in October 1950, with a further 2,600 tons from Stettin in Germany. The following month 8,000 tons came in from Stettin, from Gdynia in Poland and Rouen in France. The sharing of these large consignments was the beginning of the gradual process by which the twenty or so coal merchants in 1950 eventually amalgamated into seven, and finally combined to create Coal Distributors Ltd in 1973.

These changes must have altered the thinking of the board. The four vessels in the fleet were valued at £78,000, but their future was difficult to see. The *St Fintan* was not a good buy: it had been intended to work a Dublin–Isle of Man–Silloth ferry and cargo service, but this never made money. There was a loss of £3,541 in its first year (1949), £7,248 in 1950 and £3,330 in 1951. To add to the miseries of the venture, in November 1950 the vessel was detained in Douglas, Isle of Man, following the discovery of contraband on board. A false deck had been fitted in the forepeak, and a thriving trade in goods such as butter, ham and nylons—which were still rationed in Britain—was being carried on. As soon as she docked in Douglas, a 'black gang' of Customs searchers from Liverpool rushed on board, evidently acting on a tip-off. The *St Fintan* was released after lodgement of £2,500 with the London authorities. The board minutes noted drily: 'it is understood that no case could be made against any member of the crew up to the present'. The *St Fintan* was sold in July 1951.

The board was still faced with the problem of whether to invest or divest in shipping. It was clear that larger ships carrying enormous cargoes were the trend of the future, but there were serious questions to be asked about the long-term future of the trade. Since 1913 the flow of coal and the value of the Shipping Department had been intensely vulnerable to national and international events over which the company had no control. Already by 1950 Ireland was importing £36 million worth of fuel oils (as against £8 million worth of coal).[6] The domestic coal market might seem secure, but the same could not be said for industrial users. The following year the fleet made a loss of £7,286, and the *St Kenneth* was sold. In 1953 the last steam ship, *St Mungo,* was sold to the Hammond Lane Foundry for scrap, leaving only the motor vessel the *St Eunan.* This was sold in turn in 1958.

One factor that must have shifted management's attention away from the traditional shipping/coal configuration was the rise and rise of the 'Iron Department', as it was still traditionally called. Until the 1940s this had been a profitable, but relatively small, part of the business.

After the war it began to make more profits than the Coal/Fuel departments (see Table 6.2).

It was clear that the Iron Department was thriving. In its meticulous way the firm began to explore the gross profit contribution of the elements of the department. At first there was the simple division between the Iron Department proper and the Iron Workshop, which was a metal fabricating shop from where, as the *Souvenir Booklet* published in 1946 boasted, 'we can supply anything from a needle to an anchor'. By 1950 the accounts subdivided the Iron Department into separate sections. Over half of the department's sales came from Section 'B', which was responsible for bar iron and steel. This was also the most profitable section, with a 16 per cent gross profit (see Table 6.3). The weakest profit contribution came from the Cement section. Since this market was heavily controlled both in terms of sources of supply and sales price, it managed a gross profit of only 1.6 per cent on sales of £86,000. Although the gross profit figure had improved somewhat by the beginning of the next decade, cement was still the weakest performer in the department (see Table 6.3).

The 200-page Heitons hardware catalogue of the mid-1950s gives a detailed image of the products sold by the department at this time. It is divided into three. Unfortunately no prices are given. It starts with sections 'B' and 'C': metals and cement. The index covering these sections starts at aluminium and asbestos and runs through cement, fence posts, rolled steel joists, lead, manhole covers, cast tool steel, steel sections, wheelbarrows and wire netting. There was even a small place preserved for hoops and horse-shoes, among the very first of Heitons' lines in the Iron Department. The hardware section included plumbing goods, and covered a very wide range, from bolts and cast iron baths, through door furniture, roofing felt, glass, locks, lavatory seats, lead pipes, rivets and screws, to kitchen stoves and wash tubs. The emphasis is on heavy-duty items such as grates, stoves, pipes, etc., rather than the more decorative items such as bricks, wallpapers and paints. No timber is carried.

The last section covers engineering shop goods. Anvils, bar benders, bolt cutters, callipers, electric drills, grinding wheels, hacksaws, oil stoves, steel planes, reamers, shearing machines and vices are covered in this group. In 1955, the approximate date of this catalogue, the total stock valuation of the Iron Department was £93,000 and sales were £648,000. Stock turnover (i.e. sales divided by year-end stock) varied across the sections. The best performer was the iron and steel section, which had a stock-turn of nearly ten times a year; most of the other sections had stock turns of between two and four times a year.

As the Iron Department, previously very much the junior partner, began to contribute more and more, the board gradually began to change its view of the company's core activity. Naturally, an effective new synthesis was not to be achieved overnight. For a hundred years or more Heitons had been synonymous with shipping and coal. However, the two Hewat brothers who acted as joint Managing Directors—'Mr Cecil' and 'Mr Jimmy', as they were known to the staff—divided their interests. Jimmy Hewat was always more concerned with coal: as we shall see in the next chapter, it was he who drove the developments that lead up to the creation of CDL in 1973. Cecil, on the other hand, with the manager, Edward Usher, was primarily responsible for developing the iron side. Sid Kane remembers how he would introduce some new product or sales idea, and ask for a special report to be given to him every week so he could follow its progress.

In retrospect, the progression into the present configuration, in which steel stockholding and builders' merchanting are two of three components of the business, seems almost inevitable. (It would have taken extreme prescience in 1955 to forecast the importance of DIY.) To the board of the 1950s and 1960s things were not so clear. No doubt the depressed and underdeveloped state of the Irish economy (at least before the Whitaker/Lemass boom initiated in 1958) greatly added to the normal difficulty of strategic planning.

The great weakness of the Iron Department, however, was its vulnerability to the business cycle. Perhaps in a search for a stable counter-balance, for ten or fifteen years the company explored a number of other avenues of possible development. One of the first was the investment in 1954 of £45,000 in a 25 per cent shareholding in Booth Poole, which was set up to assemble and distribute Morris cars. The board minute in which the decision is recorded notes that the company will have 'other interests akin to those of this company'.[7] Presumably this refers to the Engineering Department. Six years later, in another sideways move, the company invested £23,000 in a company set up to produce Smiths' Potato Crisps in Ireland. It was not, as we shall see in the next chapter, until the late 1960s that the company evolved for itself a clear strategy of long-term development, and by this time the economic climate in Ireland had changed dramatically.

Chapter 7
All is Changed 1958–1974

BUSINESS HISTORY IS LITTERED with evidence of failure. Companies that thrive in one environment can very quickly be threatened with extinction when change occurs. Once renowned names are taken over, and then sink like fossils into the dusty back pages of annual reports. Ghost factories, where hundreds worked, become refuges for vagrants and playgrounds for adventurous teenagers.

The last twenty-five years have been a particularly turbulent period in Irish business history. The companies that were incorporated with Heitons in the 1890s, and the companies that sprang into existence as a result of the Control of Manufactures Acts in the 1930s, had enjoyed a long period of calm, stolid trading. The 1970s was to mark the end of this era. Inspired equally by confidence and cash, an aggressive breed of corporate engineers (of whom the best known are Michael Smurfit and Tony O'Reilly) shook the foundations of the gentlemanly business world. The change was most marked in the very largest Irish companies. In the list of the fifty largest industrial companies published in *The Irish Times* in 1966, nos. 1 and 3 are Cement and Roadstone respectively, no. 2 is W. & H. M. Goulding, no. 4 is P. J. Carroll, no. 5 is the Hely Group, no. 6 Sunbeam Wolsey, no. 7 Unidare, no. 8 Ranks (Ireland) and so on.[1] Heitons ranked no. 35, a little above T. & C. Martin and Glen Abbey. Jefferson Smurfit, whose name was misspelt, ranked no. 45. Many of these companies have fallen, often for no more fault than a certain complacency. As the BSE crisis showed, a market that seemed as secure as the Sunday roast can suddenly be decimated.

The freedom given to the corporate raiders followed the shake-up of the Irish economy initiated by Ken Whitaker and Seán Lemass in 1958/9. These economic reforms were themselves a direct response to the continuing weakness of the Irish economy. For those with vivid memories of the struggle for independence it was depressing to see 40,000 young people a year deciding to leave the country, as they did in the 1950s. Irish income per head was half that of Britain or Denmark, and one-fifth that of the United States. At the same time there was a much higher rate of unemployment than in other countries, and significant underemployment on the land. Between 1949 and 1956 Irish GNP grew 8 per cent, as opposed to 42 per cent for the other developed economies. (Britain, to whom Ireland's economic wagon was firmly linked, managed only 21 per cent.) No wonder so many ambitious young Irish people emigrated.

The old men in government lacked the will to initiate serious economic improvement. Any kind of planning smacked of socialist, communist ungodliness. Even when this obstacle was got over, de Valera himself took scant interest. After congratulating Whitaker on the 1958 Economic Plan, he characteristically added: '— but there are more important things'. Equally characteristically, de Valera claimed that there was nothing new in the Whitaker/Lemass proposals. As he told one researcher, 'we set out those policies in 1926 at the formation of Fianna Fáil'.[2]

The rest of the world thought there was a great deal that was new about the new economic plan. By good luck the publication of the plan coincided with a boom in the European economy, which it allowed Ireland to benefit from. The new policies reduced restrictions on foreign investment, cut back reliance on protective tariff barriers and prepared the economy for free trade. In hindsight, however, it is curious to see the reliance that Whitaker put on the agricultural sector,

Table 7.1: *Sources of Energy Consumption (Republic of Ireland)*

	Unit	1960	1965	1972
Coal and coke	(000 tons)	1,570	1,346	837
Gas	(m cubic metres)	160	184	200
Oil	(000 tons)	1,010	1,648	3,634
Electricity	(m kWh)	2,160	3,691	6,857
Turf	(000 tons)	1,397	2,097	3,907

Source: Coal Prices Advisory Board *Report of Enquiry into the Coal Trade* 1975

which he saw as the engine to draw Ireland Inc. forward—only about 25 pages out of 200 in *Economic Development* are devoted to industry, as opposed to 80 pages to agriculture.

Whatever the exact web of cause and effect, there is no doubt that the new departure signalled a major change. By 1963 the economy was growing at an unprecedented rate: the Stock Exchange index had shot up to 252 from 94 at the beginning of 1958; manufacturing output was 30 per cent up on 1958, and the ESB was pumping out 50 per cent more electricity than it had in 1958. Motor car sales were up to 31,700 a year (in 1932 that had been the total number of cars on the road). As Garret FitzGerald wrote at the time, 'the outlook of the people has changed gradually, but radically, from one of cynicism and near despair to one of confidence and self-assurance. This psychological breakthrough is of far greater importance than any purely economic achievements.'[3]

Although the firm's Iron Department benefited greatly from the new prosperity, Heitons was faced with the steady erosion of its traditional core business. From 1.6 million tons of coal imported in 1960, demand fell to 1.2 million tons in 1970, and continued to drop thereafter. The reduction was most marked among bulk buyers. Gas coal sales dropped from 320,000 tons to a mere 43,000; demand for steam coal fell almost as fast, as industry switched to oil and electricity. There was some consolation in the domestic demand for coal, which held more or less steady. By 1972 the household market was estimated to account for 720,000 tons out of the total usage of 837,000 tons. This was, of course, an extremely seasonal market, without the counterbalance of industrial sales in summer. Coal suppliers, however, insisted that supplies be delivered summer and winter, so by October stocks were very high, and coal merchants across the country were praying for wintry weather to start soon and last long. Although sales of 700,000 tons, which represented retail sales of about £10m, were by no means to be ignored, less than a quarter of domestic expenditure on fuel and light was now on coal. Few people can have been confident of any growth, particularly when it was reported that all-electric houses, without chimneys, were being built all over Dublin.

To meet the changing demand for coal products, in 1959 Jimmy Hewat developed the Handipac, which was a bag of pre-screened coal in handy sizes. Previously coal had always been delivered loose. The drayman lifted sack after sack from his cart and shot the coal down into the cellar, leaving the empty sack on the ground so that the householder could check the number delivered. From time to time minutes of the Staff Committee recorded acrimonious letters (and very occasionally threats of law suits) from women who felt the draymen had short-changed them in some way.

The Handipac was a creative response to a changed demand, and a

Table 7.2: *Returns on Loose Coal and Handipac (1962)*

	Loose coal	Handipac
Sales (tons)	116,976	2,528
Income (£)	825,184	26,343
Gross profit	42,734	3,488
Gross profit %	5.2	13.2
Sales per ton	£7.05	£10.40
Profit per ton	£0.36	£1.38

Source: Heitons' Archive: Private Ledger

belated introduction of the techniques of branding and pre-packing to the coal business, techniques that had been introduced to tea, sugar and similar products in the late nineteenth century. Although most kitchens and heating systems were powered by oil or electricity, many householders liked the glow and welcome of a real fire, but without having to store large quantities of coal. The many modern houses and flats that simply had no coal storage facilities were also a growing market. The Handipac came in three sizes—14 lb, 28 lb and 56 lb (14 lb is 6.3 kg)—of which the smallest was by far the most popular, accounting for three-quarters of sales. A key point of the product was that the coal was thoroughly screened beforehand, so the householder got an absolute minimum of slack. The Handipac undoubtedly met a need, selling nearly 300,000 units in 1962. As a pre-packed, branded product, a premium price could be charged, which meant that profit per ton on Handipacs was nearly four times that of loose coal (see Table 7.2).

The new product was a great success. The innovation was swiftly copied by other coal merchants, including the Cork merchants Suttons at the urging of Tony O'Reilly, then working as assistant to the Chairman before moving to Bord Bainne.[4] However there was no long term future for coal. Other cleaner, less bulky forms of heating such as electricity, oil and gas were preferred. Like the proverbial buggy-whip manufacturer in the 1920s, Heitons had to find something else to do.

We have seen in the previous chapter that the firm took a couple of false steps before settling down to its present strategy. The first was to invest in Booth Poole, which assembled Morris motor cars. The second, in the late 1950s, was to invest in Montpelier Products, which was set up to clean, wash and bag potatoes. Unfortunately, the concept was some twenty years ahead of the market and ran into problems. The potatoes available were not of a sufficiently uniform shape to be suitable for mechanical washing. Furthermore the washing process reduced the shelf-life of the potatoes, and Irish consumers were used to potatoes that lasted. Montpelier did not survive, although the bagging idea was the genesis of the successful Handipac concept.

The Montpelier factory was then used to produce Smiths Crisps in Ireland, but this dabble in the fast-moving consumer goods market was also short-lived. In a letter dated November 1965, the Chairman Jimmy Hewat explained some of the difficulties that the company, which employed sixty people, was experiencing. The core problem was the supply of suitable potatoes. Unlike the parent company in Britain, the Irish firm was not permitted to import potatoes from Cyprus. The firm was therefore completely dependent on Irish farmers, who preferred to gamble on the current market price rather than be tied to contract delivery. As a result the quality and price of potatoes, which at best had too high a moisture content, varied greatly. Very light winter demand, cost-cutting competition in the market place and problems with retailers not storing the product properly all compounded the difficulties. The control of Smiths, which had always been at arm's length, was taken over in 1966 by W. & R. Jacob, and Heitons' remaining holding was sold to Smiths (UK) in 1968.[5]

Another misdirection was the purchase in 1965 of R. Ferguson Peacocke Ltd, an engineering company with a small factory in Denzille Lane, which was a large purchaser of steel from the firm. This company specialised in metal engineering assignments for architects, including church furnishings, candelabra (for the Shelbourne), balustrades, etc. Among its projects were seats for the new Abbey Theatre. When it was taken over, Ferguson Peacocke owed Heitons a large debt, and the board considered that its activity might 'broaden the basis of our activities on the manufacturing side, and we hope to develop exports'. Despite a lot of board time, the working methods of the two firms could not be brought into line, and the firm was sold in the late 1960s.

None of these investments was for large sums of money—the holding in Montpelier Products was only £10,000 (£80,000 in 1996 terms). Although they seem now to be distractions from the right path, they do reflect an interesting aspect of the way the firm saw itself. These were all in their way premium brands. Heitons had always exuded characteristic concerns with honest dealing, with reliability, with tradition. It prided itself on its almost military cleanliness, in, for instance, the spick and span appearance of its drays (in the 1930s winning their section at the RDS three times in succession). As we have seen, there was constant reinvestment in plant and equipment, constant attention paid to the decorative order of the premises, constant discipline in keeping the ledgers immaculate. In looking for new investments, therefore, the board was always attracted by companies that reflected the way it saw itself—selling respected brands with high product quality and good trading possibilities.

In fact the new direction for the firm was to come not from these outside ventures, but from within. Over the years the Iron Department had always been the junior partner, and a board given to reading the *Harvard Business Review* might have been tempted between the wars to divest this activity and stick to the 'core business'. Undiversified companies, however, pay for the benefits of specialisation with increased vulnerability to external changes.

The two departments, coal and iron, were run quite separately. They even had different business hours, with the coal people opening their office half an hour later. Despite its wide stock range, which turned over quite slowly, the Iron Department always made regular profits, and Cecil Hewat, Chairman and Managing Director from 1935 to 1963, had maintained it as his particular interest, working closely after the war with the manager, E. S. 'Ted' Usher who, in recognition of his importance to the firm, became a member of the board in 1958. The coal business was largely managed by Jimmy Hewat. It was he who maintained the reputation of the firm in that market and also among his fellow coal merchants.

In the late 1940s and 1950s a boom in house building gave Heitons exactly the opportunity it needed. Since the population of Ireland was virtually static—it had been 2.960m in 1951 and was 2.978m in 1971—one would have imagined that the demand for house building was easily satisfied. However, these static totals conceal a major shift of population to Dublin. Between 1951 and 1966 100,000 people were added to the population of Dublin, putting a great strain on the rather poor housing stock. (As late as 1961 30 per cent of houses in Dublin had no hot water, and 20 per cent had no indoor lavatory.[6]) Naturally not many houses had been built during the war period, so when materials became available again after 1948 there was a tremendous surge of building. Heitons responded to this market demand by rapidly developing its builders' providers section in George's Quay. This business was largely wholesale, serving both city and country merchants. In the fourteen years between 1946 and 1960 over fifty thousand houses were built in the Dublin area, not to mention the churches, factories and other facilities required to accommodate the new population. In the following fifteen years, between 1961 and 1976, a further eighty thousand houses were built. According to the 1991 Census, just over half of the current housing stock in Dublin was erected in this thirty-year period.

In the mid to late 1960s the board approved a completely new strategy for the development of the non-coal business. As drawn together in a paper delivered to the board by Richard Hewat, Jimmy's son, who had recently joined the firm from the accountants Stokes Brothers and Pim, it predicated a major shift in customer base. The newly active IDA were pushing the idea of regional development, and with the prospect of membership of the EU, farmers were beginning to enjoy a new prosperity. The board took the view that developments in transport and product packaging were such that the local wholesaler was vulnerable. So Heitons was going to break the basic business rule, 'never compete with your customers', and supply the building and allied trades directly. This is an archetypal moment in business history, when the prime source of a product range (importer or producer) decides to cut out the middleman and approach the market directly. It is often a moment of major vulnerability. If the firm has correctly estimated the value chain from producer to final consumer, the gains can be enormous, not only by reducing transaction costs and bringing the wholesalers' profits into the group, but also by being able to use the direct contact with the market to develop new product lines. On the other hand, the demands of new stockholding require-ments, new cash and credit controls, and new management pressures can seriously damage the business. Heitons was to experience (and survive) in the mid 1970s some of the trauma that this strategic shift can cause.

The first step in carrying out this new strategy was to widen the capital base. The limited company had been launched in 1896 with 12,000 ordinary shares, of which Sir Malcolm Inglis and William Hewat held 5,597 each. When the two founders died in 1900 and 1902, their holdings were considerably broken up. Sir Malcolm's hold-ing was sold in over ninety parcels, of which the largest (3,000 shares) was administered as a trust by the Bank of Ireland, before being sold some years later in a further twenty parcels. The largest of this group, 1,340 shares, was bought by a stockbroker, William Kennedy Rogerson, in 1915. He sold on in 11 parcels between 1916 and 1917, the largest tranche, 400 shares, going to Cecil Hely of Orwell Road, Rathgar, whose two children inherited them in 1944. This process completely scattered the Inglis holding. When the company wanted to appoint Jimmy Hanna to the board in 1956, it had difficulty in acquiring the necessary qualifying shares. Cecil Hewat wrote to Mrs Jeannie Geoghegan, Sir Malcolm's daughter, who had 713 shares, the largest holding outside the Hewat family or the board, to ask if she would be prepared to part with some. She politely declined.

The only centripetal force in the shareholding was the Hewat fam-ily, which quietly added to its holding over fifty years. William Hewat II (Managing Director 1901–35) started with a relatively modest hold-ing of 200 shares in 1896. By persistent small purchases—sometimes of only five shares at once—he built this to a personal holding of 2,400 shares (20 per cent of the company) on his death in 1935. To this were added 3,600 shares from his uncle William Hewat I which had been held in trust. The combined holding of 50 per cent of the company then descended to William II's six children, including Cecil and Jimmy who became successive chairmen. The policy of regularly increasing the family holdings was carried on, with the remarkable effect that by 1963 the Hewat family interests owned 59 per cent of the ordinary shares; the next largest holding was the Harper family, with 18 per cent.[7]

The first step in the new departure was to increase the authorised share capital by the creation of 36,000 ordinary shares paid for by the capitalisation of £180,000 out of reserves. This was done in 1963. The next step was to raise capital on the Stock Exchange. In 1965 the authorised capital was raised to £750,000, and £240,000 was raised from the public.

With this war chest, Heitons was able to make a major step forward. The practical implications of the new policy were:

—the creation of a nation-wide chain of supply centres, with A stores in large towns and B stores in smaller ones, in response to the growing demand from non-Dublin building, industrial and agricultural customers;

—a greatly increasing product range, developing cash sales business, aiming at builders rather than wholesalers.

As it happened, the old-established builders providers McFerran & Guilford were just at this time looking for a partner, having been stung recently by a venture in steel windows. Net profit had slumped by 38 per cent in three years, and the current credit squeeze was widely expected to cause problems for the building trade. (Dockrells, T. & C. Martin and Brooks Thomas all reported reduced activity and profits in 1966/7. T. & C. Martin went into liquidation in 1968.) McFerran & Guilford possessed strengths in several aspects of the trade that Heitons were not deeply involved in, notably plumbing and timber. They also had an established connection with numerous small building firms in Dublin. The two businesses had of course been well aware of each other from the beginning, being dockland neighbours. McFerran &

Guilford traced their history back to 1878, when John McFerran began importing building materials from Britain and Scandinavia. In 1907 his son Robert was joined by Sidney Guilford, and in the 1930s new premises were acquired in George's Quay, Poolbeg Street and Luke Street. In the 1940s they established a depot in Ringsend, and in the 1950s a timber yard in East Wall Road. In the mid 1960s they built a splendid new showroom in Tara Street, with a ground floor especially designed to show off the plumbing suites. This gleaming facility with its large plate glass windows attracted much attention, not all of it welcome. The story is still told in the firm of how, when the first double bath was proudly displayed for the world to see, the local parish priest called to complain of the firm encouraging immorality in this way!

Heitons was planning to rent a floor of this building, but in the course of the negotiations about the lease a more intimate relationship was mooted. In May 1967 this came to pass, and the two firms merged. Thomas Heiton became the holding company and was renamed Heiton Holdings; McFerran & Guilford became the trading arm, now called Heiton McFerran. Although this was a straightforward takeover, with Heitons' shareholders ending up with three-quarters of the equity, a deliberate, self-conscious and, in retrospect, probably unnecessary effort was made to present the result as an equal merger between the two companies. The new board was carefully balanced, with joint managing and sales directors. Jimmy Guilford became joint managing director of Heiton McFerran, with special interest in timber. He was also a director of Switzers. Keith McFerran, who had been in the Royal Navy during the war, joined the board of Heiton Holdings, and was mainly concerned with clay goods, bricks, firebricks and sewage pipes. He was also a director of the *Irish Independent*. Despite this thought and effort, in practice there was tremendous difficulty in combining the two systems, partly due to the very different types of customers that each brought in. Heitons had tended to specialise in wholesale customers, while McFerran & Guilford, who had several depots in Dublin, were much more heavily involved in direct selling to the building trade. The combined firm became the second largest builders' providers in Dublin after Brooks Thomas.

The following year the firm opened its new Cork depot, and took over the Limerick timber merchants Morgan McMahon. Morgan McMahon had been founded fifty years before, and had a turnover of £700,000 with gross profits of £50,000. They employed 86 people in Limerick and 24 in their Dublin depot. Both of these deals were midwifed by the firm's accountants Craig Gardner, with Guinness and Mahon and the newly founded Investment Bank of Ireland. Heitons was now the largest builders' supplier in Ireland, and was continuing to expand.

By the end of 1971 the shares were quoted at 75p, having been 46p five years before. Profits in 1966 were £65,000 and by 1971 they had climbed to £385,000. In 1971 the company bought John Myles, a small builders' supplier in Ballyshannon, and much more significantly a 15-acre site on the Naas Road planned to be the central stockholding site, which could provide modern cost-effective stocking and handling facilities. In the cramped and old-fashioned premises in George's Quay there was no possibility of very much expansion or indeed automated handling of large loads. As a result all the Iron Department's product, including steel girders weighing half a ton or more, had to be man-handled on to the customers' lorries, most of which were too large to get inside the building, so had to be loaded in the road. At this time traffic conditions around the George's Quay site had become very difficult. Double yellow lines inhibited parking, and when they didn't Heitons' staff found themselves paying their customers' parking fines!

In the heated, nervous atmosphere generated by the Troubles in the North, there was also a security aspect. Bomb scares were a regular occurrence in Tara Street, though the nearest the firm got to actual damage was a suspicious incident on the afternoon of 17 May 1974, when an appalling series of bombs in Dublin and Monaghan—for which no warning was issued—killed 31 and injured 150 people. At about 4 o'clock a man with a heavy Northern accent called by the Poolbeg Street depot and asked: 'What time do the workers get out?' Many in Heitons believe there was a connection between this enquiry and the subsequent bombing. Although most of the firm's customers still regarded the Naas Road as half-way to Galway, a move was clearly desirable.

It was clear that the builders' providers and metal sides of Heitons' activity were going from strength to strength. The future of the coal side was less assured, and the newspapers regularly speculated about when, if and how Heitons would dispose of its coal interests. The seventeen main coal merchants in 1955 had been reduced, mainly by amalgamation, to seven by 1973. The trade exhibited a curious combination of intense competitiveness at the sales and operational level, and great cooperation in purchasing and labour bargaining. There were still a number of yards on either side of the Liffey, most being small, under-utilised and inefficient. Margins were tight and new customers were few. None of the companies was above a little industrial espionage to check the quality of coal being delivered to its rivals, or to undercut prices. Sid Kane, who served as ship's agent from 1958 to 1974, vividly remembers a surreptitious expedition on to one of Dohertys' boats to check that the jointly purchased cargo was being fairly shared, for, while retreating, he twisted his foot into a rail, and broke it.

During the 1960s an increasing proportion of coal imported came in large cargoes from Poland. This trade had been tentatively initiated by Tedcastles in the 1950s, and there had indeed been some press comment on the undesirability of trading with such a godless, communistic country. (A year or two before Archbishop McQuaid had done his best to prohibit a proposed football match between Ireland and Yugoslavia.) The earlier cargoes were imported through Irish Coal Importers Ltd, a trade association formed in the early 1930s, with its origins in the old Dublin Coal Merchants' Association. The individual firms

A 'breaster' whose job was to lift sacks of coal either on his chest from ground to lorry or on his back from lorry to ground. The 10 stone bag (64 kilos) probably weighed more than he did. (Photo: Cliff Eager)

The last of the old steam cranes in action in Custom House Dock—the 'canter' guides the coal into the lorry. (Photo: Cliff Eager)

Three Managing Directors:
(Above) Jimmy and Cecil Hewat
(Left) Jim Hanna

Occasionally these 30-ton cranes tipped over, and had to be set upright again by even larger cranes.

The company's last vessel, the St Eunan. *During the Second World War, as a British registered ship, she carried a small gun on the poop deck (roughly where the crewman is standing in the stern). The 'H' on the funnel was the characteristic Heiton's identifier.*

Advertising on the Rathmines tram before the First World War

Some eighty people, though no spouses, attended the 1952 staff party in the Hotel Victor Killiney—in the front row are the organising committee, (l–r) Lil Fitzpatrick, Arnold Carroll, Sylvia Timmons, Jimmy Hewat, Tom Spencer, Ted Usher and Raymond Murphy.

Jim Hanna, Jimmy Hewat, Keith McFerran and Thomas V. Murphy at the announcement of the merger

Jimmy Hewat (front row centre) with a Polish coal delegation—other Dublin coal trade leaders pictured include Harry Lamb, MD of Donnellys (front row left), Tom Sheridan, Chairman Irish Coal Importers (front row right), Ruben Mackenzie of Mackenzies (2nd row, 2nd left), John Reihill of Tedcastles (3rd row first left).

W. E. D. Hewat, Director
1923–47

J. Denham Macalister, Secretary
1925–47

The view from the Secretary's
office in 37 George's Quay

The firm bought J. J. Carroll in 1944, largely in order to increase its wartime coal import quota, and continued to use the name for trading purposes until the 1960s.

Handipacs being delivered to a small grocer

The last phase of shipping: (Above) Paddy Hughes, Stevedore (centre) and Sid Kane (Ship's Agent) discuss the raising of a cargo from the Senator Possehl. (Below) The Norwegian ship Havgast, whose pregnant stewardess caused some problems when she discharged herself from hospital

Morgan McMahon's timber yard in Limerick

The purpose-built Cork office in 1968

Each yard employed only three or four permanent yardmen, taking on 20 or more 'regular' casuals, who worked from September to March, and 'temporary' casuals as needed. (Above) With the pipe is one of the firm's characters, Owen Hoare, a filler who worked all his life in the yards. (Below) Custom House Dock staff (l–r) (not known), Mattie Berrigan, Jim Burns, Manager, Cliff Eager, Assistant Manager. Mattie Berrigan joined the firm as a messenger boy, and remembered carrying money from the yard to George's Quay in his cap during the Troubles. (Photos: Cliff Eager)

The last years at George's Quay, during the building of the Talbot Bridge

The new premises at Ashfield, on the Naas Road, in 1973 in the early stages of construction

The old-style builders' providers—Heitons branches in Bray (above) and Ringsend (below) in the early 1970s.

The beginnings of DIY—Poolbeg St (above) and Letterkenny showrooms (below) in the late 1970s

Ronnie Guilford (left) and Richard Hewat (3rd left) at the press reception for the opening of the new showrooms in Tara Street in 1978

'A new name on the Irish scene—Ireland's most comprehensive builders' suppliers organisation' was how Heiton McFerran was announced to the public in 1967. Ironically it was timber that caused most trouble in the difficult days of the early 1970s.

At the Staff Party in Leopardstown, in 1996 to celebrate the centenary

Retired staff members (l–r) Sid Kane, Wally Aylward and Alex Duke

(L–r) Mick Dunne, Vinny O'Brien and Jimmy Gainsford

Staff from Bond Road
(L–r, standing) Róisín O'Reilly, Imelda O'Sullivan, Tom O'Sullivan, Rose Ryan, Michael Flanagan
(seated) Ann Flanagan, John O'Reilly, Gladys Martin, Tommy Martin, Denis and Diane McKenna

Directors and Secretary in 1996

(L–r) Leo J. Martin, Charles E. Craig, Stephen O'Connor (Chairman)

(L–r) Peter Byers, J. Richard Hewat (Managing Director), John Bourke

(L–r) Niall V. G. Carroll, Vincent O'Doherty, Mary O'Callaghan (Secretary), Martin E. Simmons

shared the cargo and took it in turn to organise discharge.

Closer amalgamation between the larger firms was increasingly likely. In the early 1960s a combined group from the industry toured the great ports of Europe to look at how facilities for importing 40,000 tons at a time were handled. In 1966 the *Evening Press* caught wind of one of a series of discussions involving Heitons, Donnellys, Tedcastles and Dohertys. These were held in some secrecy, in the country, or in obscure places in Dublin. Nothing came of this however, since the companies could not agree on the relative shares.[8] By 1972 coal imports were down one-third on the 1966 figure, and in June the National Price Commission effectively forced the trade's hand. While allowing an application for an increase in price, it declared that 'when we receive the next application for an increase in the price of coal we would expect that the present inefficiencies had been reduced'. This threat to future revenue concentrated minds. Led by Jimmy Hewat who, like William Hewat II, was greatly trusted by his fellow-merchants—a compliment not lightly handed out—the industry went back to its discussions.

By September the coal merchants had agreed to combine. They also accepted an offer by the Dublin Port and Docks Board to create a new facility in Ringsend. Despite the declining market, the merchants invested £1m in this facility. Coal Distributors Ltd (CDL) was operational by December 1973, although the new terminal at Ringsend did not get fully under way until March 1974. Under the terms of the

Table 7.3: *Coal Imports by Source*

	Total (000 tons)	(of which)	UK %	US %	Poland %
1961	1,771		63	11	11
1966	1,312		30	24	32
1971	1,021		16	4	74

Source: Report of Enquiry into the Coal Trade (1975)

agreement, each of the companies entered a covenant that for ten years they would not 'carry on or help or assist or be engaged or concerned or interested in any coal merchants' trade or business' in the Dublin area. The actual importation of coal would continue to be organised by the individual companies. At this point Heitons' direct sales of coal, which had been its mainstay for more than 150 years, was over, although the firm continued to enjoy dividends from its holding in CDL, which traded very successfully for many years.

No time was allowed, however, to digest this historic moment. In October 1973 the Yom Kippur Arab-Israeli war broke out. The members of OPEC first of all raised the price of oil from $3 to $5.12 a barrel, and then, in order to put pressure on Israel, began to embargo supplies to the United States. These two actions were apparently unconnected, but the OPEC countries quickly realised how profoundly the West relied on their oil. In December they turned the screws several notches, raising the price to $11.65 a barrel. The OPEC communiqué announcing this rise smugly pointed out that 'all those children of well-to-do families who have plenty to eat at every meal . . . will have to rethink all these advantages of the advanced industrial world. And they will have to work harder.'[9] For a country like Ireland, which had cheerfully increased its dependence on imported oil until it was providing three-quarters of its energy requirements, this was a disaster.

The effect on fuel prices was immediate. The fuel component of the Consumer Price Index shot up from 152 in November 1973 to 197 in February 1974 (1968 = 100). However, it took some time before the effects filtered through to the economy as a whole, and in September 1974 Jimmy Hewat was able to announce a 94 per cent increase in profits, which broke the £1m mark for the first time. Turnover was up 30 per cent to £13m. Ominously, stocks were also up, from £0.4m to £1.4m. These results included three months of the recent acquisition, hardware and engineers' providers Stephen Stokes Ltd of Limerick. However, there were straws in the wind. In his Chairman's report, Jimmy Hewat commented:

there is much pessimism in Business generally, which is caused by prevailing conditions and the uncertainty of what lies ahead . . . if the difficult trading conditions experienced within the past two months were to continue during the remainder of the year there is no doubt but that our earnings would be severely affected, bearing in mind particularly the present high cost of financing stocks.

His words were to prove a considerable understatement.

Chapter 8
A Managed Transition 1975–1996

GLOBAL COAL SUPPLIES were dogged by all the mayhem of the restless twentieth century—problems far outside the company's control, including strikes, international disputes and wars. At another level, however, the coal market was more or less isolated from the economic cycle, and the systems for supplying that market were well honed. Now the company was to embark on a different road, one that was to have many ups and downs over the next few years.

The establishment of Coal Distributors Limited (CDL) in 1973/4 marked a major shift in Heitons' activities. There was also a shift in key personnel, as Jim Hanna became Chairman and Richard Hewat, Jimmy's son, became Managing Director at the end of 1974. These two were now presented with one of the most demanding challenges to business management—the complete transition from one well-known and understood product base to another. As well as the obvious differences of products, markets and customers' habits, there was a profound change in the economic factors that the firm's management had now to consider. Until the move to oil and electricity, coal consumption had been only slowly affected by macro-economic events. Building activity, on the other hand, is directly proportionate to business confidence and interest rates. If the cost of money is too high, return on building investment becomes unattractive, and activity slumps. Construction plans also react very quickly to adverse conditions. In a matter of months conditions switch from favourable to unfavourable, leaving builders' suppliers dangerously over-stocked. From the calm of selling a product largely isolated from rapid shifts in economic activity, Heitons was now committed to riding the dragon of the economic cycle.

The time was not propitious for such a change. In 1974, as the effects of the Yom Kippur War and the OPEC countries' oil price rise filtered through the economy, Heitons was suddenly given a dramatic lesson in how much more important the level of interest rates was to a firm supplying the building trade than to a coal importer. The new Chairman, Jim Hanna, was obliged to announce the first loss the company had made since 1879. In his review of the year issued with the annual report dated April 1975, he told shareholders that the previous year had

> probably been the most difficult in the history of your company. In the corresponding period last year the demand for many building materials was simultaneously high in virtually every country resulting not only in higher prices but also in orders being placed many months in advance of delivery dates to secure supplies. Trade was buoyant . . . during [1974/5] the recession deepened with sales falling off and margins tightening in a highly competitive market: the private house-building sector of the construction industry, despite assurances to the contrary from high places, came practically to a standstill, while in other areas many projects and developments were abandoned or deferred.

On a turnover of £12.8m (slightly down from the previous year), a profit of £1.3m had turned into a loss of £1m. A key problem was that, encouraged by the success of the previous year, the firm had invested heavily in timber stocks, buying forward to ensure supplies. This, of course, was standard practice, with which the two McMahon brothers, Denis (based in Limerick) and Brendan (based in Dublin), were very familiar. Brendan had joined the Heiton McFerran board in 1973, and from 1974 was broadly in charge of timber buying, though a company called Heiton Timber had been established to centralise buying as far as possible.

In 1975 the building trade virtually came to a stop, leaving suppliers such as Heitons, Dockrells (then part of Tony O'Reilly's Fitzwilton Group) and many others, holding excessive stocks. Media comment later suggested that Heitons and the other firms that were equally badly caught should have anticipated the downturn, but the feeling in the company is that the suddenness of the downturn, deriving as it did from external international events, could hardly have been foreseen. Not only was there a trading loss after interest of £0.14m, but it was necessary to write a substantial amount off timber and other stocks. Given the likely demand from the building trade, these were now much too high, in Heitons' case partly because a six-week strike in 1974 had reduced sales. The banks were especially concerned with the holdings of timber.

Immediately before the Yom Kippur War, heavy demand from Japan in particular had pushed world timber prices up, amd many forward contracts were at those levels. As soon as the oil price rises took effect national and international demand dried up very quickly. Unlike the other hardware products, timber has a finite shelf life. It can only be stored for a certain time before it deteriorates. When the building market collapsed, the banks took fright and insisted that £856,000 of existing stocks and future contracts be written off by Heitons. At the same time the company's bank borrowings shot up from £800,000 to £3.2m. A director from Allied Irish Investment Bank, John Bourke, joined the board. For the next two years there was a constant strain on the new Managing Director as the firm attempted to juggle the demands of the banks, to regulate stockholding and to squeeze margins in an intensely competitive period. Perhaps surprisingly, Richard Hewat himself remembers this stressful period as 'quite exhilarating in its own way'.

The downturn, however, signalled the start of ten tense and difficult years. Just at the time when the firm's exposure to the business cycle was greatest, the Irish economy entered an extremely rough

Table 8.1: *Riding the Dragon: Heitons' pre-tax profit (£000)*

	Turnover	Pre-tax profit	CPI (1970=100)
1970	n/a	372	100
1975	12,820	(912)	186
1980	28,659	931	360
1985	27,489	(339)	642
1990	55,201	2,603	755
1995	118,000	4,010	855

Source: *Annual Accounts*

period. Since Ireland imported 70 per cent of its primary energy requirements, mostly in the form of oil, the massive price rise was bound to have a dramatic effect. Economic growth rates slowed down markedly in 1974–6, and after a brief respite in 1977–9, led by an expansionary government, plunged into further decline with the second oil price rise of the early 1980s.

Builders' merchants or providers supplied three products to the building trade. The first was branded goods, of which there was an increasing flow; the second was commodity goods (such as glass, steel, timber); and the third was credit. The latter was extensive—in a special report on the industry (June 1979) the National Prices Commission wrote: 'It is commonly acknowledged amongst builders, as well as builders' providers, that the latter are in part financing the building industry'. Each of the products carried its special risk. Branded goods and other items such as readymix concrete, bricks and pipes were very often supplied direct to the market by manufacturers or their agents, making the firm vulnerable to the classic margin squeeze position of the middleman. In the growing agricultural sector, the co-ops supplied a considerable proportion of farmers' needs. In 1977 it was estimated that builders' providers as such supplied only 42 per cent of the total value of building materials sold to builders. The prices of commodity goods were extremely volatile, being highly susceptible to slight shifts in world supply and demand. Furthermore, since large users can source supplies directly from the originating coun-

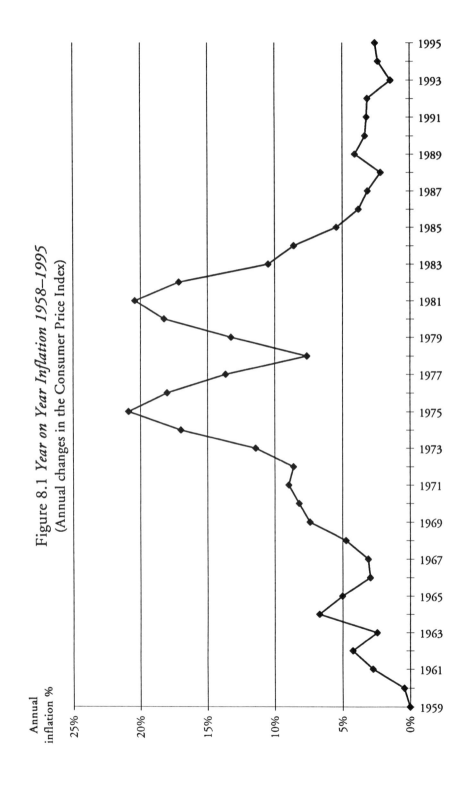

Figure 8.1 *Year on Year Inflation 1958–1995*
(Annual changes in the Consumer Price Index)

try as soon as the savings outweigh the transaction costs, there is a natural limit to order size. Finally, in a world in which bankers were extremely conscious of the risks involved in the market, credit was an expensive commodity to supply.

The builders' providers' market in the 1970s went through an extremely difficult period. Great pressure was put on the Heitons' financial management skills, as inflation shot to 21 per cent in 1975, came down to 7.6 per cent in 1978 and then shot up again to 20 per cent in 1981. These wild variations particularly affected three areas in which the builders' providers business was vulnerable. As a labour intensive industry, wages rates were crucial, as were the economic cycle and the prices of raw materials. The report by the National Prices Commission put the industry in a wider context:

> Since the 1950s the volume of building has increased enormously. This has been accompanied by an increase in the number of firms in the trade and in turn by increased competition . . . with the increase in competition has come an increase in the complexity of the business. The number of products has expanded, and new materials are constantly being added. In the 1970s flexible exchange rates added another dimension to the difficulties involved in purchasing in an industry subject to marked fluctuations in demand. Some recent economic changes have also worked to the disadvantage of the longer established firms. The increased prosperity of the agricultural sector, and the policy of encouraging industrialisation in the less developed parts of the country have encouraged demand in areas remote from the urban areas where the longer established builders' providers are concentrated . . . meanwhile labour costs have escalated. The upshot of these fundamental changes in the structure of the industry has been a period of flux, with several firms disappearing, others changing the nature of their business and others merging or entering associations to ensure survival. On the other hand, new firms have emerged as major factors in the trade and there have been significant British investment in some areas of the business.

Luckily for its long-term future Heitons had committed itself to the development of the Ashfield site on the Naas Road. The removal from the cramped premises in George's Quay enabled Richard Hewat and his managers to put in place those crucial improvements to operating systems and staffing levels that would permit survival. It also meant that the steel stock-holding side of the business in particular could grow unrestrained by the physical limitations of George's Quay. During the 1960s and 1970s a gradual change had come over the market. Not only was more steel in larger unit sizes being demanded, but the demand now came direct to Heitons from the end-user rather than via the traditional country merchants. In George's Quay virtually all the handling was done manually—in Ashfield the overhead cranes could lift up to four tons whereas the manual limit was about half a ton. Not only could the new warehouse service a wider range of customers, but it could do so with fewer staff. There were redundancies, but since the older men generally preferred not to move to the Naas Road, nearly all of them were voluntary. The new warehouse, with its six overhead cranes, was the biggest purpose-built facility of its kind in the country. With this equipment, the manager of the department, Charles Craig, was able to respond to the growing demand for steel products. Over time the Steel Department began to develop sales beyond the traditional building trade into other non-building uses.

The 1976 accounts showed a much smaller loss on a reduced turnover, but Jim Hanna was able to strike a cautiously optimistic note:

> in the early part of the year under review [1975/6] the difficult trading pattern experienced in the previous year continued with low activity and pressure on margins. During the last four months however volumes and margins did improve . . . Dublin and the surrounding counties have been more severely hit by the recession than some country areas and our new branch in Waterford, which commenced trading in June 1975, exceeded its budget for the year.

The next four years, 1977–80, were a period of reasonable growth, with overall profits helped by healthy contributions of over a million pounds from Coal Distributors Ltd. Coal sales were benefiting from the government attempt to reduce the national commitment to oil by encouraging the sale of solid fuel burners. Having been scorned for so long, coal was now back on the agenda; indeed, as Hanna put it, 'coal had now regained its place as a leading source of energy'. The increased use of coal gave the firm an agreeable each-way bet on the weather—if the weather was generally bad, building activity was re-

Table 8.2: *Property Assets in 1976*

County	Status
Dublin	
Ashfield, Naas Road	Freehold
2–16 Tara Street	Freehold/Leashold
George's Quay	Freehold
1–4 Luke Street	Freehold/Leashold
39–42 Poolbeg Street	Freehold/Leashold
South Lotts Road	Leashold
Grand Canal Dock, Ringsend	Leashold
Bond & Promenade Road	Leashold
West Pier, Howth	Leashold
Cumberland Street, Dun Laoghaire	Freehold
Townsend Street	Freehold/Leashold
Cork	
Tory Top Road, Ballyphelane	Leashold
Kinsale Road, Black Ash	Freehold
Donegal	
Port Road, Ballyshannon	Freehold/Leashold
Kildare	
Eyre St Newbridge	Leashold
Limerick	
Dock Road	Leashold
Mulgrave Street	Leashold
Cecil Street	Leashold
Henry Street	Leashold
Waterford	
Cork Road	Freehold
Wicklow	
Castle Street, Bray	Freehold

Note: These properties were professionally valued in 1974 at £3,628,531.

duced, but on the other hand coal usage went up, and vice versa. The major shadow on the horizon, however, was inexorably rising wages costs. Annual inflation, which had peaked at 21 per cent in 1975, went back to 14 per cent in 1979. Wages, driven by the National Wages Agreements, began to climb. On the other hand, the board was happy to note a greatly increased level of commercial and industrial building activity.

The following year, with inflation at 18 per cent, the firm began a long rationalisation programme that was to cost £1.4m in redundancy payments in four years. A steady attack had to be made on costs at all levels. At the heart of this was a computerisation programme put in place by the finance director Louis McSherry. Until then the enormous number of individual calculations relating to the ordering, invoicing and selling of the 12,000 items the firm carried had been done by comptometer and calculator. (The purchase of the firm's first comptometer in the late 1940s was a great event. This large machine, with its banks of keys and complicated mechanical workings, cost as much as a small car. As befitted its cost, it was carefully locked away every night. Special training was required to perform the thousands of elaborate invoice calculations—such as '2 tons 6 hundredweight 3 quarters of steel at £120 16s 3d a ton'—that were processed every day.) The introduction of computers allowed the firm greatly to reduce its clerical staff.

In his report to the shareholders in 1975 Hanna had described the key factors influencing demand for the firm's products. These were: the level of activity in the construction industry, the state of business confidence generally, which in turn governed the number and size of capital investment projects and the availability of money. With inflation back to record levels, interest rates high, and business confidence low, it was no wonder that the outlook for the building industry, and consequently for Heitons was less than rosy.

Two bright spots, however, showed themselves. The first was Richard Hewat's well-timed sale of the George's Quay property, just before commercial property prices in the city collapsed. The sale ended a 130-year connection with this historic site. It was here, facing the Custom House, where Thomas Heiton himself and his partner Gilbert Burns had originally established the firm in the 1850s. The site was sold to Irish Life for £1.73m, realising a profit of £660,000. The proceeds of the sale went to reduce the firm's borrowings, thus lowering interest charges by some £200,000 a year. The profit from this sale and the contribution from CDL of £689,000 turned a trading loss in 1981 into a profit.

The second bright spot, at least at first, was the establishment of Home Grown Timber Ltd. The firm was anxious to diversify—it had looked at glass, at electrical goods and at fish-farming—and this project aimed to use locally grown timber in place of some of the £37m worth imported from Scandinavia and other countries. Two-thirds of the timber imported into Ireland was used for construction and housing, so there was a good congruence with Heitons' other interests. Furthermore, the IDA was extremely keen on this project, seeing it as a classic piece of import substitution.

A great deal of research was done into the best plant and machinery available. A consultant from Sweden advised the consortium, which included Heitons and Coal Distributors Ltd. Work started on the construction of a mill in Fermoy in 1979, and it was anticipated that when it was in full operation, as much as 40,000 cubic metres of high–quality kiln-dried timber would be produced every year. In 1977 the country imported 373,000 cubic metres of softwood. There was, however, a potential snag. The world price for timber is extremely volatile. To be a success, the mill at Fermoy needed to be in regular operation, with a constant flow of product passing out to Irish users. However, since there was no possibility of a building contractor paying more for timber than the prevailing European price, the success of the project depended on the willingness of the Department of Forestry to sell timber recognising those prices. Although the Department from the beginning refused to give any promises to that effect, the consortium felt that the influence of the IDA would be sufficient to stimulate a pricing structure aligned to world prices.

Unfortunately the Department, which had an effective monopoly of supply of home-grown timber, took the non-commercial view that they had no need to sell timber at reduced prices. So when the world price of timber fell after the second major oil price rise in 1981, they refused to supply logs at then prevailing prices. Although the quality of the product was well-received in the industry, sales could not be made at the higher prices, and in July 1983 a receiver was called in, with the loss of 75 jobs. Heitons was estimated to have lost £500,000 on the venture. Jim Hanna, whose strong-minded, straight-talking personality had gained him great respect as a negotiator with the dock labourers, put the blame bluntly where he felt it belonged in his 1983 Chairman's report.

> The necessity for the appointment of a receiver . . . is a severe blow not only for the Group but also for the development of the saw-milling industry in this country. Established in conjunction with the IDA as an integral part of the strategic plan to maximise the return to the economy from the utilisation of the country's timber resources, the company has achieved a new image for the quality of well prepared native timber. It must be stated that the apparent failure of the Department of Fisheries and Forestry to recognise that this is a new industry geared specifically for import substitution which requires fresh commercial consideration was a major cause of the problem.

For Richard Hewat the collapse of Home Grown Timber 'was one of my biggest disappointments—there was so much about the project that was right for Heitons and for Ireland'.

In June 1984 Jim Hanna, who had been with the firm for 59 years, decided to retire. His outstanding service included a period as Company Secretary (1947–56), as joint Managing Director (1964–75) and as Chairman (1975–84). Richard Hewat now became Chairman and Managing Director, handing over the chairmanship to Diarmuid Quirke in 1992. As luck would have it, just as there had been a loss announced in his first year as Managing Director, he was obliged in his first year as Chairman to report a small loss on a diminishing volume of activity. The building industry continued to suffer from the poor state of the national economy; among the sore points was the enormous VAT rate of 35 per cent charged on many materials used for repair and maintenance of property which in turn encouraged the black economy at the expense of legitimate businesses. The vagaries and reductions in the public investment programme were another problem.

The accounts would have looked worse than they did had it not been for another property coup. In 1983 Richard Hewat sold the firm's city-centre showrooms in Tara Street to the Irish Press Group for £80 a square foot, a remarkable price at the time. As *Business and Finance* commented shortly afterwards: 'Hewat obviously saw the Irish Press coming. They would have been able to buy office space in Dublin 4 for that price. Exactly what the Irish Press is up to is anyone's guess.'[1] This wide-ranging article examined the future for Heitons—including a glancing comment to the effect that 'there are many arguments against keeping the top management position in a company in the same family for such a lengthy period and there are even stronger arguments against this when it is a public company'—but took the largely favourable view that despite the lack of dividends and the lack of confidence in the building industry generally, the share was a 'hold'.

The following year (1985) marked both the end of the long period of retrenchment and the beginning of a resurgence. Activity in the building trade was still depressed, largely because of the taxation regime, and therefore turnover remained constant at just £27m for four successive years. Behind this screen however, the firm was becoming much leaner and fitter than it had been. A second wave of computerisation enabled the builders' suppliers side of the business greatly to improve its efficiency. The special expertise that the firm developed in computer-based internal systems and controls later came to be recognised as a major asset.

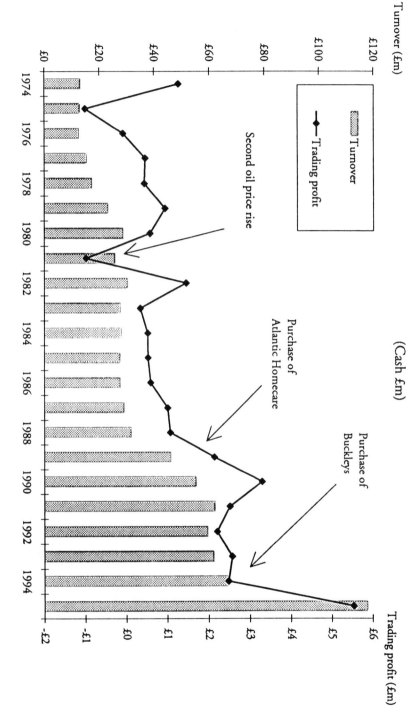

Figure 8.2 *Heitons Turnover and Trading Profit 1974–95*
(Cash £m)

Yet in some ways the company was still quite old-fashioned in its style. The two main executive directors, Richard Hewat and Ronnie Guilford, were referred to by the staff as 'Mr Richard' and 'Mr Ronnie'; the marketing approach was somewhat staid, even dull. On the builders' supply side, which was Ronnie Guilford's speciality, there was a great opportunity for streamlining. The purchase and sale of builders' products were in the hands of area specialists. A builder who required more than one item, as was typical, would call first at one cubby-hole, then another, for each of the product types. The clerks behind the counter would be knowledgeable in their particular area, and having discussed the order, would disappear to the large warehouse to recover the goods required. The new system swept away the cubby-holes (described as being like those of an old-fashioned pawnbroker's in appearance), and enabled the builders to buy all their requirements from a single clerk, who, with the computer on the counter, was able to service all their needs in one transaction. The new system enabled the division to increase its range of items stocked, and yet maintain tight control, so that there are now some 30,000 product lines stocked, compared to 12,000 in 1980.

The restructuring had, however, taken its toll on the balance sheet, and in 1985 the management was faced with the choice of trading out of the cash problem, which would have taken years, or injecting more capital. Richard Hewat decided to seek new investors. Although trading was still quite difficult, and there were constant harassing cash flow problems, the company did have an attractive package to sell. It had good property backing, with seventeen premises in twelve locations around the country; the economy was at last beginning to turn, and the company had completed four-fifths of a rationalisation programme. With help from the Standard Chartered Bank in London, five institutions—Allied Combined Trust, Investors in Industry, Irish Life, Standard Life and Allied Irish Holdings—were found to take substantial holdings in an issue of 7.5 per cent Convertible Preference Shares, giving an increase of £2.5m to the balance sheet.

This crucial development in the recent history of the company was combined with a strengthening of the management—in particular by the recruitment as Finance Director of accountant Leo Martin from Switzers in 1986—and further changes in operational systems. There was a sharpening of management focus on cash flow and margin levels, and the reductions in staff effected with some pain over the previous years left the firm in a position to make the most of the improvements in the economy that were about to come. The result has been a steady increase in shareholder value ever since. In the late 1980s turnover climbed steadily from £27.4m in 1986 to £55.2m for the year ending 30 April 1990. By this time the firm was in an excitingly different situation from that of the beginning of the decade. Over the previous five years it had grown steadily, regaining confidence in itself. Its 372 employees were now paid an average of £12,950 a year.

In 1990 the firm had just completed two acquisitions, one of which, Atlantic Homecare, was a step in a new direction. The DIY market, which had its origins in the United States in the 1950s and had migrated to Britain in the 1960s, was slow to reach Ireland. Only in the late 1970s and early 1980s did it take off in any serious manner, no doubt stimulated by the extremely high rates of VAT then prevailing. The pioneer and market leader in the 'shed' business, selling DIY and homecare products from large warehouse-type buildings stocking everything from nails to bathrooms, from rakes to roofing materials, was Hollington, trading under the name Atlantic Homecare. At the time of purchase, Atlantic's turnover had gone from £2.8m in 1986 to £6.5m in 1989, and profits had increased threefold in the same period.

This acquisition brought the management expertise of Atlantic's founder, Martin Simmons, into the group. The physical assets consisted of three major stores in Dublin and a further four Atlantic Homecare stores operating under franchise in Dublin and Cork. Strategically, this acquisition provided an opportunity to smooth the impact of the business cycle for the group. As we have seen, reliance on the building business had exposed the group to the ups and downs of the cycle in an often uncomfortable way. The DIY market was much less exposed—if anything, people spend more maintaining and developing their homes in depressed times. Furthermore, the customer base was quite different, and this was a cash business, operating at full pitch seven days a week, with no credit worries.

Not all the developments in the late 1980s worked well. On 21 March 1988 the company bought Gilbert T. Bell, a steel stockist in Birmingham, and a year later Gloucester Steelstock. The first year's turnover in this venture was £9.5m, almost 10 per cent of the company's total sales, but the returns were not satisfactory, and a builders' providers business was developed in the Birmingham premises to increase profitability. Unfortunately, the basis of the expansion was completely undermined by a major shift in the conditions of the steel market. Not only were conditions in the UK economy unattractive, but also the major steel mills had decided to expand vertically into steel stock-holders, making the position of an independent stock-holder untenable. A quick decision was made to liquidate the investment in Birmingham, where turnover had collapsed from £10m to £6.4m, and the company refocused its attention on the island of Ireland.

Although more publicly visible, the Atlantic Homecare division was much less important to the company than the builders' merchants side. The DIY stores added a turnover of £6.5m to Heitons' existing sales of some £50m. The bulk of turnover and profit therefore derived from the trading of the builders' merchants and steel merchanting units. For thirty years the company has steadily pursued the objectives established by Richard Hewat in the mid 1960s in his paper to the board referred to in Chapter 7. These were the creation of a nationwide chain of supply centres and a greatly increased product range. As the IDA pushed forward its regional industrial policy, and as farmers made increasing use of new building materials, this policy became more and more important. All of the present locations

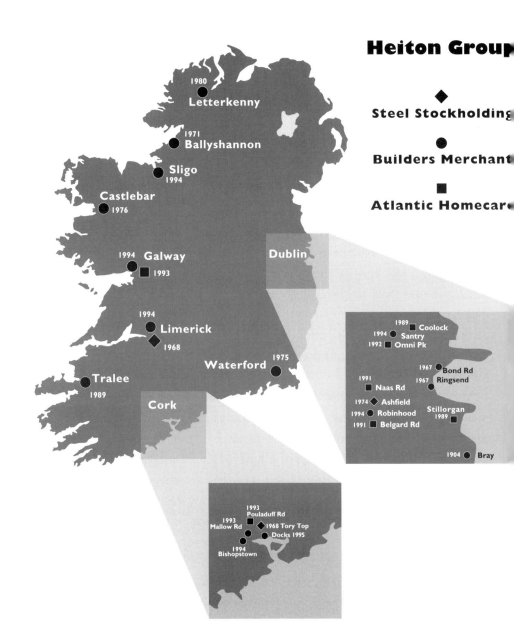

Heiton Group

◆ Steel Stockholding

● Builders Merchant

■ Atlantic Homecare

1980 Letterkenny

1971 Ballyshannon

Sligo
1994

Castlebar
1976

1994 Galway
1993

1994 Limerick
1968

Waterford 1975

Tralee
1989

Dublin

Cork

1989 Coolock
1994 Santry
1992 Omni Pk

1967 Bond Rd
1991 1967 Ringsend
Naas Rd

1974 Ashfield
1994 Robinhood Stillorgan
1991 Belgard Rd 1989

1904 Bray

1993
Pouladuff Rd
1993 1968 Tory Top
Mallow Rd Docks 1995
1994
Bishopstown

(with the exception of Bray) have been acquired since that policy was laid down. Even Bray, which was acquired in 1904 and operated until 1968 as a coal yard, was radically developed thereafter. The present range of builders' merchants and steel supply centres rings the country, running through the major population centres, with the sole exception of the north-east.

In pursuit of this long-term policy of establishing a nation-wide coverage of outlets, in 1989 the firm bought McCowens of Tralee, which was run by Frank King, Chairman of the Kerry GAA, a local celebrity. The store was very well respected in the area, with a lot of local loyalty, not least because of the current successes of the Kerry GAA squads. In the past McCowens had done a very large business in wild game. *The Fowler in Ireland* records that in the very cold 1880/81 season they bought 16,481 gamebirds, including 9,264 snipe, 2,021 woodcock, and 1,861 widgeon. Our Victorian ancestors, apparently, were happy to kill and eat almost anything—other birds traded included brent geese, curlew, duck (pintail and diving), grebe, grouse, oyster-catchers, partridge, pheasant, plover (golden and green), rail, redshank, teal and waterhen.

In the purchase of such well-established stores, there was a delicate job to be done of developing the stock and the sales approach in line with Heitons' nation-wide ideas, but without alienating the local customers, who were still demanding products such as horseshoes and dog muzzles, for which there is not much call on the Naas Road.

The purchase of the Buckleys Group in 1994 was a particulary important step forward in pursuit of Hewat's longterm plan. Buckleys, with two outlets in Dublin and others in Cork, Limerick, Galway and Sligo, brought sales of around £35m into the group. It made Heitons the largest builders' merchants group in the country. Described by Goodbody Stockbrokers as making 'brilliant strategic sense', the acquisition also brought a different focus. Buckley's primary merchanting concentration was in housebuilding, while Heitons was better known for its relationships with major contractors on flagship projects, and its architectural and other niche specialisms.

Four-fifths of Buckleys' turnover of £34m turnover was from housebuilders. Goodbodys further noted that

> apart from products and markets, the businesses of Heiton McFerran and the recently-acquired Buckleys are complementary in several other ways. There is virtually no geographical overlap. In addition, Heiton has an expertise in the area of computer systems and controls, while Buckleys is well recognised for the strength, experience and depth of its management. Synergies arising from the acquisition are internal—in the areas of purchasing, administration and working capital management.
>
> The timber business is a further example . . . Heiton McFerran has traditionally been a major importer and distributor of timber, both hardwood (25 per cent) and softwood (75 per cent). Buckleys, by virtue of its housebuilding focus, is also a large-scale supplier of timber, although it is virtually all softwood. This year timber volumes are expected to be 100,000 cubic metres. through both Heiton McFerran and Buckleys and revenue should be around £20m.

By 1995, therefore, the Builders' Merchants Division had come a long way from the bar iron and tyre hoops of the original Thomas Heiton. Today it sells some 30,000 separate lines, including everything from nails and plumbing goods to bricks and doors. The scale has changed somewhat also; in a single year the firm can now expect to sell some ten million bricks and 70,000 doors. It has 30 per cent of the steel stockholders' market, 20 per cent of the Irish brick market, and 22 per cent of the construction timber market. Under Leo Martin, who had moved from Finance to become Managing Director of the greatly enlarged division following the acquisition of Buckleys, the division has concentrated on broadening its market base, while at the same time developing more sophisticated marketing techniques. The sales people now spend a lot of time making presentations to contractors, securing very large contracts such as the Tyrone brick used in Blackrock Shopping Centre in Dublin. However, the firm was aware that many contractors had shifted their own business away from employing builders to sub-contracting. In some branches, 80 per cent of Heitons' business now comes from small builders, who prefer to buy their supplies early in the morning. This prevents any security problems that might arise from materials kept on-site overnight. Heitons' decision to provide a full 'bacon and egg' breakfast for these customers was a small but very attractive addition to the service.

The steel business has broadened its activities in three directions over the twenty years since the move from George's Quay. First, purpose-built warehouses were established in Dublin, Cork, Waterford and Limerick and suitable warehousing for steel in the builders' merchants stores set up across the country. Second, the range of products in the steel division now amounts to appproximately 1,000 different items. While not neglecting the small engineering shops and the traditional building requirements, sales have expanded into security fencing, machine safety meshes, and steel for all types of farm buildings as well as tubing for milking parlours. The improvements in our roadways has resulted in a demand for safety barriers, of which Heitons is the main supplier. In a curious harking back to the time when the bulk of the iron supplied was for horseshoes and tyres for horse-drawn transport, Heitons now has a thriving market in steel for lorry and tractor trailers, which use four different types of steel—plate, tubing, flat steel and channel. The latest way in which the division has expanded is in the range of buying sources. In the old days all steel was bought from Britain; now, though Britain remains the biggest supplier, steel comes from Turkey, Belgium, Spain, Finland and other EU countries.

Although there is a certain amount of value-added activity, in bending and shaping steel for instance, the policy of the division has generally been to stick to the provision of basic steel. Like all Heitons' divisions, Charles Craig's steel unit keeps a very close eye on its competitive position, pushing all the time to reach market leadership. At the moment Heitons is the biggest Irish steel stockholder in the country, with some thirty competitors.

In 1995 the Homecare/DIY division recorded a turnover of £17.1m, with 27,000 customers a week. A process of rationalisation, moving away from central warehousing to a system allowing local managers to call-off requirements directly from the suppliers, was in progress. With a focus on computer technology to improve customer service, price competitiveness and the provision of a broad range of products, the Group is conscious of the potential growth in the DIY market as a whole, for Irish expenditure per head is at the moment only about 45 per cent of the UK equivalent.

Although Heitons had moved out of the coal-selling business with the establishment of Coal Distributors Ltd in 1973, the company long retained a considerable interest in solid fuel sales. It continued to import coal for CDL, and as a large shareholder (at one time, briefly, the majority shareholder), it gained a steady flow of welcome profits. In the four years from 1987 to 1990, for instance, the firm received £2.7m from that source (the profits of Hollington over the same period were about £1m). In 1990, however, the board made a strategic decision to sell its remaining 41.5 per cent share. The mild winters, and new legislation banning bituminous coal, as well as a general intention to concentrate on what was now the core business, were key factors in this decision. For various reasons, however, it was not until early in 1995 that the firm's very last connection with coal ended with the sale of Heitons' stake in CDL.

In 1995, twenty years after the turmoil caused by the oil price rises of 1973, Stephen O'Connor as Chairman was able to report that the 738 full-time and 140 part-time employees had generated record profits of £4.8m on a turnover of £118m. The difficult times that had briefly returned in 1991/2, with high interest rates inhibiting building investment, were past, and the outlook was positive, with 'growth in the economy projected to the year 2000 and beyond, underpinned by the availability and utilisation of EU structural funds, low inflation and low interest rates'. He went on:

> the strategy for the future will be to continue to drive increasing returns from the Group's asset base for our shareholders, using our balance sheet strength and low gearing. We will undertake acquisitions and expansions, but only if they fit well with our core business and allow us to realise synergies and to maximise organic growth. We will continue

to benefit from our positive positioning in the home market and will build up the strong domestic base as a springboard for consideration of appropriate opportunities for geographic expansion outside Ireland in the medium term, if our strategic acquisition criteria can be successfully met.

In the short term, the stock market at least takes the view that this strategy will work, for the share price went above £1 for the first time during the centenary year. It will be for the historian of the next fifty years to say how well the targets are achieved in the long term.

Appendix 1
Directors and Principal Officers 1896–1996

Directors

Name	Appointed	Left	Reason
William Hewat I	14 May 1896	6 Dec 1900	Died
Sir Malcolm Inglis	14 May 1896	24 Apr 1902	Died
Frederick W. Pim[1]	14 May 1896	7 Jan 1925	Died
George Macnie[1]	14 May 1896	29 Jul 1914	Resigned
Robert Harper	14 May 1896	26 Jun 1935	Died
Robert M. Inglis	14 May 1896	5 Mar 1923	Died
William Hewat II	2 Jan 1901	15 May 1935	Died
Vivian D. Inglis	25 Aug 1902	14 Apr 1909	Resigned
Hugh Harper	12 Jan 1912	27 July 1963	Died
Hamilton Whiteside	1 Aug 1915	10 Sept 1936	Died
William E. D. Hewat	12 Mar 1923	13 Apr 1947	Died
Cecil D. Hewat	10 Jul 1925	31 Oct 1963	Resigned
James C. D. Hewat	26 Jun 1935	31 Dec 1974	Resigned
J. Denham Macalister	25 Sep 1935	31 July 1957	Resigned
Valentine A. Carroll	28 Jun 1944	10 Feb 1961	Resigned
James Hanna	14 Jun 1956	19 July 1984	Resigned
Edward S. Usher	22 Oct 1958	28 Apr 1967	Resigned
James J. Hussey	1 Nov 1963	28 Apr 1967	Resigned

Name	Appointed	Left	Reason
John H. Guinness[1]	5 Feb 1965	27 Feb 1988	Died
James H. Guilford	1 Mar 1967	17 Dec 1985	Resigned
Keith McFerran	1 Mar 1967	26 Nov 1981	Resigned
Thomas V. Murphy[1]	1 May 1967	26 Nov 1981	Resigned
Denis McMahon	27 Mar 1968	24 Nov 1977	Resigned
Ronald T. Guilford	16 Nov 1971	31 Jul 1995	Resigned
J. Richard B. Hewat[2]	16 Nov 1971		
Colm O'Rahilly	9 Apr 1974	30 Jan 1986	Resigned
John K. Bourke[1]	29 Jan 1975		
Louis J. McSherry	25 Mar 1976	31 Dec 1986	Resigned
Andrew H. Teare[1]	10 Jan 1984	25 Oct 1990	Resigned
Niall V. G. Carroll[1]	31 Oct 1985		
Leo J. Martin	3 Apr 1986		
Martin E. Simmons	25 Jan 1990		
Diarmuid F. Quirke[1]	13 Mar 1991	21 Sep 1994	Died
Charles E. Craig	1 Sep 1993		
Vincent O'Doherty[1]	1 Sep 1993		
David G. Dillon	27 Oct 1994	26 Mar 1996	Resigned
Stephen O'Connor[1]	20 Nov 1994		
Peter J. Byers	29 May 1996		

[1] External, non-executive director. Note the long gap between the death of Frederick Pim in 1925 and the appointment of the next non-executive director, John H. Guinness of Guinness and Mahon in 1965.

[2] Richard Hewat had previously been a director of the company from 1 January 1967 to 28 April 1967 but resigned on the amalgamation with McFerran and Guilford and joined the board of the trading company Heiton McFerran Ltd.

Principal Officers

Chairman

Sir Malcolm Inglis	14 May 1896–24 April 1902
George Macnie	24 April 1902–14 July 1914
William Hewat II	14 July 1914–15 May 1935
Cecil D. Hewat	22 May 1935–31 October 1963
James C. D. Hewat	17 October 1963–31 December 1974
James Hanna	1 January 1975–19 July 1984
J. Richard B. Hewat	19 July 1984–31 October 1992
Diarmuid F. Quirke	1 November 1992–21 September 1994
Stephen O'Connor	20 November 1994

Managing Director (often Joint)

William Hewat I	14 May 1896–6 December 1900
Sir Malcolm Inglis	7 December 1900–1 January 1901
William Hewat II	2 January 1901–15 May 1935
Cecil D. Hewat	9 November 1925–31 October 1963
James C. D. Hewat	4 October 1946–31 December 1974
James Hanna	6 February 1964–31 December 1974
J. Richard B. Hewat	1 January 1975–

Secretary

William Hewat II	14 May 1896–2 January 1901
Vivian D. Inglis	2 January 1901–14 April 1909
Robert M. Inglis	14 April 1909–1 March 1923
Cecil D. Hewat	1 March 1923–9 Nov 1925
J. Denham Macalister	9 Nov 1925–30 June 1947
James Hanna	1 July 1947–6 February 1964
Sidney W. Kane	6 February 1964–30 April 1988
Leo J. Martin	1 May 1988–30 June 1994
Mary O'Callaghan	30 June 1994–

Appendix 2
Heitons' Fleet

1. Sailing vessels

Albion
(8745) A brig of 146 gross tonnage[1], built New Brunswick 1838; acquired by Thomas Heiton 1847; sold to T. W. Adams, Dublin in 1880.

Syren
(35230) A brig of 170 gross tonnage, built Nova Scotia 1845 for T. Heiton. Her ultimate fate is not known.

1. *Gross tonnage* is a measure of volume, not of weight, historically based on the potential grain-carrying capacity of the vessel. *Net register tonnage* is gross tonnage less certain deductions such as crew spaces, water ballast tanks, propelling power allowance. Neither of these measures bears a direct relationship to the carrying capacity. For historic reasons harbour dues were based on gross tonnage while agents' fees and light dues (for the upkeep of lighthouses etc.) on net tonnage. Still other dues were paid on the actual cargo carried. Finally it should be noted that for safety reasons (the Plimsoll or load line) the carrying capacity in winter was less than that of summer.

The table below shows the relationship for some of Heitons' purpose-built colliers. In a converted vessel such as the second *St Fintan*, which was originally intended to carry passengers, the volume measures would bear even less relationship to the carrying capacity.

Gross Tonnage, Net Register Tonnage and Carrying Capacity

Ship	Gross Tonnage	Net Register Tonnage	Carrying capacity (tons)	
			Fore hold	Aft hold
St Patrick	648	245	400	350
St Kevin	679	259	380	350
St Mirren	557	223	290	290
St Margaret	449	191	280	240
St Mungo	402	146	200	200

North Ash

(8817) A schooner of 118 gross tonnage, built Brixham 1810; acquired by Thomas Heiton in 1860; sold to P. Kirwan, Dublin in 1888.

Eglantine

(55851) A barque of 331 gross tonnage, built Quebec 1866; acquired by T. Heiton & Co. 1880; sold to A. C. Neilsen, Norway in 1888.

2. Steam Vessels

Arbutus

(18205) A steamer of 356 gross tonnage, built Newcastle-on-Tyne 1854; acquired by T. Heiton & Co. 1880; sold to R. Taylor, Dundee in 1885.

St Kevin

(81446) A steamer of 456 gross tonnage, built by McIlwaine and Lewis, Belfast 1883; sold to Wadsworth & Co., Goole in 1894.

St Margaret

(96050) A steamer of 449 gross tonnage, built by Scott & Co., Bowling 1889; foundered off Hook Point, 7 December 1919 on voyage from Troon to Waterford with the loss of her entire crew of twelve men.

St Kilda

(96087) A steamer of 451 gross tonnage, built by J. Fullerton & Co., Paisley 1894; foundered off The Chickens, 26 February 1926 on voyage from Llandulas to Glasgow with the loss of her captain and three crew. Four men were lost.

St Mirren

(104548) A steamer of 557 gross tonnage built by J. Fullerton & Co., Paisley 1894; foundered off The Chickens, 26 February 1926 on voyage from Llandulas to Glasgow with the loss of her captain and three crewmen.

St Olaf

(105989) A steamer of 568 gross tonnage, built by J. Fullerton & Co., Paisley 1896; lost in collision with *SS Voltaic* off Holyhead, 1 December 1900 on voyage from Treport to Liverpool. No loss of life.

St Kevin
(111030) A steamer of 679 gross tonnage, built by J. Fullerton & Co., Paisley 1900; sold to Mann McNeal & Co. in 1915.

St Patrick
(117515) A steamer of 648 gross tonnage, built by J. Fullerton & Co., Paisley, 1903; foundered off Start Point, 26 November 1912 on voyage from Dieppe to Weston Point with the loss of her captain and four crewmen.

St Fintan
(119140) A steamer of 368 gross tonnage, built by Scott & Co., Bowling 1904 and launched as *Plover* for David MacBrayne; acquired by T. Heiton & Co. Ltd as *Loch Aline* from Burns and Laird Lines Ltd in 1947, converted to carry general cargo and renamed *St Fintan*. Sold in July 1951 to British Iron and Steel Corporation.

St Mungo
(123128) A steamer of 402 gross tonnage, built by Scott & Co, Bowling in 1907, torpedoed and sunk by U-boat on 2 May 1917 with the loss of her entire crew of twelve men.

St Mungo
(144968) A steamer of 448 gross tonnage, built by Ailsa Shipbuilding Co., Troon 1920; sold to Hammond Lane Metal Co. in November 1953 and broken up.

St Fintan
(144973) A steamer of 495 gross tonnage, built by Ailsa Shipbuilding Co., Troon, 1921; bombed and sunk by German aircraft 22 March 1941 off The Smalls on voyage from Drogheda to Cardiff with the loss of all on board. Nine men were lost.

St Kenneth
(146415) A steamer of 681 gross tonnage, built by Scott & Co., Bowling 1924; sold to H. Craig & Co., Belfast in 1953.

3. Motor

St Eunan
(115054) A motor vessel of 436 gross tonnage, built by Ailsa Ship-building Co., Troon 1937; sold to J. Psimenos, Greece in May 1958. Her new owner renamed her *Prassonisia.* She was lost with all hands some months later, during a storm in the Aegean.

Note: The last of the Heitons Ships' Masters were:

Captain Owen Keefe from Arklow, Master of the *St Mungo*
Captain William Roberts from Wales, Master of the *St Kenneth*
Captain James Stewart from Dublin, Master of the *St Fintan*
Captain William McGuinness from Dublin, Master of the *St Eunan*

Appendix 3
The Hewat Family in Heitons

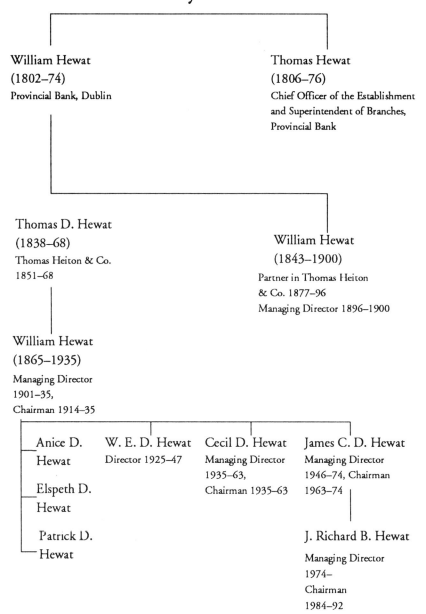

William Hewat
(1802–74)
Provincial Bank, Dublin

Thomas Hewat
(1806–76)
Chief Officer of the Establishment
and Superintendent of Branches,
Provincial Bank

Thomas D. Hewat
(1838–68)
Thomas Heiton & Co.
1851–68

William Hewat
(1843–1900)
Partner in Thomas Heiton
& Co. 1877–96
Managing Director 1896–1900

William Hewat
(1865–1935)
Managing Director
1901–35,
Chairman 1914–35

Anice D.
Hewat

W. E. D. Hewat
Director 1925–47

Cecil D. Hewat
Managing Director
1935–63,
Chairman 1935–63

James C. D. Hewat
Managing Director
1946–74, Chairman
1963–74

Elspeth D.
Hewat

Patrick D.
Hewat

J. Richard B. Hewat
Managing Director
1974–
Chairman
1984–92

Endnotes

Notes to Chapter 1

1. [Attributed to J. Denham Macalister] *Heitons 1896–1945* Dublin: privately printed 1946 p 21
2. G. N. Wright *An Historical Guide to the City of Dublin* 2nd ed. 1825
3. F. Engels *Condition of the Working Class in England in 1844* translated and edited by W. Henderson and W. Challoner, Oxford: Blackwell 1958 p 40
4. Calendar of State Papers (Irish 1599–1600) p 102
5. Wm Petty *Writings in Political Economy* 'The Irish Excise' p 589
6. J. U. Nef *The Early History of the British Coal Trade* Cambridge: Cambridge University Press 1937 vol 1 p 100
7. J. Swift 'Letters upon the use of Irish coal' in *Works of Jonathan Swift* ed. Sir Walter Scott London: Bickers 1883 vol vii p 212
8. John Finlay, quoted in Lawrence Adamson *A Letter to the Rt Hon the Lord Mayor of the City of Dublin on the Abuses in the Coal Trade* Dublin, 1827 RIA Halliday Collection 1405. This pamphlet provides a lively picture of the conditions in the coal trade in the 1820s by a man who was personally involved in importing coal from Whitehaven.
9. Captain Spargo, quoted in J. MacRae and C. Waine *The Steam Collier Fleets* Wolverhampton: Waine Research Publications 1990 p 99
10. The law relating to coal is summarised in L. MacNally *The Justice of the Peace for Ireland* Dublin: Fitzpatrick 1812 vol 1 pp 432–40.

It should be noted that these are not general United Kingdom Acts, but were specific to Dublin.

11. E. Bullingbroke *The Duty and Authority of Justices of the Peace and Parish Officers for Ireland* Dublin: George Grierson 1788 p 170
12. Adamson *A Letter to the Rt Hon the Lord Mayor*
13. Quoted in A. Peter *Dublin Fragments* London: Murray 1927
14. P. Somerville-Large *The Irish Country-House* London: Sinclair-Stevenson 1995 pp 169, 222
15. T. Holme *The Carlyles at Home* Oxford: Oxford University Press 1979 p 148
16. The details of how the iron was used are based on G. Sturt *The Wheelwright's Shop* Cambridge: Cambridge University Press 1923, and E. Estyn Evans *Irish Folk Ways* London: Routledge and Kegan Paul 1957 ch 13

Notes to Chapter 2

1. J. U. Nef *The Rise of the British Coal Industry* London: Cambridge 1937 vol 1 p 70
2. H. O'Hara *Report on the Supply of Fuel in Ireland* Dublin 1866 p 18
3. D. Landes *The Unbound Prometheus* Cambridge: Cambridge University Press 1969 p 97
4. Elizabeth Smith 'Unpublished Diaries' 27 May 1853
5. C. Ó Gráda *Ireland: A New Economic History 1780–1939* Oxford: Oxford University Press 1994 p 309
6. Nef *The Rise of the British Coal Industry* p 392
7. 67 xvi 333
8. W. Runciman *Collier Brigs and their Sailors* London: T. Fisher Unwin 1926 pp 206–7
9. Ibid. pp 86–7
10. Select Committee on the Coal Trade 1830 (496) xlix199 mf 53.36
11. J. Mokyr *Why Ireland Starved* London: Allen and Unwin 1985 p 154
12. O'Hara op. cit. p 20
13. *Report of Proceedings of a Commission of Inquiry into the Local Charges on Shipping within the Port of Dublin* Dublin: 1855 pp 15, 26

14. J. MacRae and C. Waine *The Steam Collier Fleets* Wolverhampton: Waine Research Publications 1990 p 99
15. After September 1854 the voyage accounts were recorded elsewhere, perhaps to allow a more detailed analysis such as was used later. In the frugal manner of the firm, the leather bound ledger in which these first voyages were recorded was later used to record the balance sheets of the new partnership of J. Malcolm Inglis and William Hewat between 1877 and 1896, which is no doubt why this fragmentary record has survived.
16. Heitons' Archive: Stock Book —this information and the debtors listing are evidently working summaries for inclusion into a balance sheet.
17. Heitons' Archive: Stock Book
18. Heitons' Archive: Voyage Book—a similar breakdown was given in the following year's accounts, but thereafter the stocks are given in total only.
19. As the then President of the Dublin Chamber of Commerce, he was knighted by Queen Victoria after her visit to Ireland in 1900.
20. L. Cullen *Princes and Pirates: The Dublin Chamber of Commerce 1783–1983* Dublin: Chamber of Commerce 1983 p 78

Notes to Chapter 3

1. M. Healy *The Old Munster Circuit* London: Michael Joseph 1939 p 73
2. Heitons' Archive: Board Minutes I 333
3. M. McCarthy *Five Years in Ireland 1895–1900* Dublin: Hodges Figgis 1901 pp 70–1
4. Conal O'Riordan *Adam of Dublin* London: Collins 1920 p 11
5. Owen Spargo and Thomas Thomason *Old Time Steam Coasting* Wolverhampton: Warne Research 1982 pp 10, 14
6. Heitons' Archive: Board Minutes II 50
7. Heitons' Archive: Board Minutes II 19
8. Heitons' Archive: Board Minutes II 169
9. Heitons' Archive: Board Minutes II 209
10. Heitons' Archive: Board Minutes I 336
11. Heitons' Archive: Stock Book
12. Heitons' Archive: Board Minutes 11 May 1898
13. R. Nesbitt *At Arnotts of Dublin 1843–1993* Dublin: A. & A. Farmar 1993 p 22

Notes to Chapter 4

1. E. Somerville and Martin Ross *Dan Russel the Fox* London: Methuen 1911 ch 16
2. *Irish Worker* 4 November 1911, quoted in Curriculum Development Unit *Divided City—Portrait of Dublin 1913* Dublin: O'Brien Press 1978 p 52
3. Quoted in L. Cullen *Princes and Pirates: The Dublin Chamber of Commerce 1783–1983* Dublin: Chamber of Commerce 1983 p 83
4. *Freeman's Journal* 2 September 1913
5. P. MacAonghusa and L. Ó Reagain *The Best of Connolly* Cork: Mercier 1967 p 21
6. T. Zeldin *France 1848–1945* Vol 1 Oxford: Oxford University Press 1973 pp 236–7
7. *Freeman's Journal* 6 November 1913
8. E. O'Connor *A Labour History of Ireland 1824–1960* Dublin: Gill and Macmillan 1992 p 68
9. K. Kearns *Dublin Tenement Life —An Oral History* Dublin: Gill and Macmillan 1994 p 26
10. Heitons' Archive: Board Minutes II p 179
11. J. O'Brien *'Dear Dirty Dublin' A City in Distress 1899–1916* California: University of California Press 1982 p 225
12. Heitons' Archive: Board Minutes II 25 September 1914, p 267
13. Heitons' Archive: Board Minutes II 16 August 1916
14. Heitons' Archive: Board Minutes II p 339 14 September 1917
15. Heitons' Archive: Board Minutes II p 361
16. Heitons' Archive: Board Minutes II p 376

Notes to Chapter 5

1. G. D. H. Cole and Raymond Postgate *The Common People 1746–1938* London: Methuen 1945 p. 563
2. *Irish Coal Committee Report* 1919 p 4
3. Heitons' Archive: Staff Committee Minutes 22 September 1915
4. A. D. Chandler *Strategy and Structure* Cambridge, Massachusetts: 1962 ch 3
5. *Freeman's Journal* 16 August 1923

6. *Dáil Debates* 26 May 1925
7. *Dáil Debates* 11 July 1924
8. *Freeman's Journal* 25 August 1923
9. E. O'Connor *A Labour History of Ireland* Dublin: Gill and Macmillan 1992 p 119
10. B. Mitchell *Abstract of British Historical Statistics* Cambridge: Cambridge University Press 1971 p 224
11. William Cunningham, who was senior partner of Craig Gardner 1969–71, saw many such cases. He told the author that in his opinion the most serious failure of the accountancy profession in the 1940s and 1950s was not to urge proper financing of pension schemes. See also *The Legendary Lofty Clattery Café: Bewleys of Ireland* (Bewleys: Dublin 1988) by Tony Farmar for the results of one such unfinanced scheme.

Notes to Chapter 6

1. D. Ó Drisceoil *Censorship in Ireland 1939–45* Cork: Cork University Press 1996 pp 3–7
2. N. Monsarrat *The Cruel Sea* London: Cassell 1951 p 151
3. B. Share *The Emergency: Neutral Ireland 1939–45* Dublin: Gill and Macmillan 1987 p 11
4. F. Forde *The Long Watch* Dublin: Gill and Macmillan 1981
5. Heitons' Archive Board Minutes 30 September 1941
6. *Statistical Abstract 1951*: if Heitons had noticed the forthcoming importance of oil, the Central Statistics Office certainly had not. Motor spirit, and gas and fuel oil are still listed under the heading 'Oil Seeds, Oils, Fats etc.'.
7. Heitons' Archive: Board Minutes 4 August 1954

Notes to Chapter 7

1. *The Irish Times* 8 November 1966—companies were ranked in order of capital employed.
2. J. McCarthy *Planning Ireland's Future* Dublin: The Glendale Press 1990 p 51
3. T. Farmar *Ordinary Lives* Dublin: A. & A. Farmar 1995 pp 164–5
4. I. Fallon *The Player* London: Hodder and Stoughton 1994 p 109
5. The continuing dominance of certain families in Irish business was

displayed by the ten-man board of Jacobs at this time, which contained a Jacob, a Pim, two Bewleys and a Guinness—see their advertisement in *The Irish Times*, 4 May 1966.

6. *Census 1961*: In the country an even more frugal comfort pertained. Only one-tenth of farm dwellings had either a fixed bath or a hot water tap, just over a fifth had piped water, and less than a third had any sanitary facilities beyond a bucket in an outhouse.

7. Heitons' Archive: Register of Members 1896–1963—the practice of numbering each share enables us to trace the path of each holding. The Hewat family clearly agreed with Michael Smurfit's well-known saying, 'Equity is blood'.

8. *The Irish Times* checked the story with Jimmy Hewat. With careful *suggestio falsi* he told them that the first he 'saw' of it (meaning of course the story) was when he spotted the newspaper placards. *The Irish Times* misreported his statement as a denial that any such meeting took place.

9. A. Sampson *The Seven Sisters* London: Hodder 1975 pp 265–71

Note to Chapter 8

1. *Business and Finance* 16 February 1984

Index

Account of Coals Imported into Ireland,
   1818, 16
accounts, 35, 40, 48, 51, 76, 89,
   1995, 144–5
   debtors, 25, 26–7
   losses, 125–6, 135
   profits, 30, 65–6, 75, 136
   rents, 76–7
   return on capital, 77–8
Admiralty Court, 41
Aiken, Frank, 87
Albion, 17, 18, 23–4, 149
Aliens Office, 103
Alliance Gas, 25
Allied Combined Trust, 137
Allied Irish Holdings, 137
Allied Irish Investment Bank, 126
Arbutus, 29, 150
Arnotts, 48
Ashley, Thomas, 3–4, 5, 7, 14, 21, 22
Atlantic Homecare, 138–9
Austen, Jane, 11

Ballast Office, 20, 21, 24
Bank of Ireland, 97, 116
Barry, David, 78
Belfast, 16, 20, 33, 46, 52
Belgium, 88, 143
Bell, Gilbert T., 139
Bewley, Samuel, 22
Bewleys, 25, 34
B&I Steam Packet Company, 25
Blackrock Shopping Centre, 142

Booth Poole, 107, 112
Bord Bainne, 112
Bourke, John, 126, 147
Boyle, Charles, 47
Brady, Alice, 61
Bray, Co. Wicklow, 35, 43, 50, 64, 74,
   141
Breen, Dan, 68
Bridge Street, 96
Brooks Thomas, 117, 119
Brown Thomas, 25
Buckleys Group, 141
Builders' Merchants Division, 114–15,
   117–19, 124–6, 135, 137, 139,
   141, 142
   Buckleys Group acquired, 141–2
   difficulties, 126–30
Bulfin, 33
Burns, Gilbert, 4, 21, 24, 34, 133
Business and Finance, 135
Butterworth, McArthur Nash and Co.,
   27
Byers, Peter J., 147
Byrne, Alfie, 78

Carlyle, Mrs, 12
Carroll, J. J., 96–7
Carroll, Niall V. G., 147
Carroll, P. J., 108
Carroll, V. A., 97, 146
Castlecomer coal, 74
Catholic Emancipation Act, 1829, 11
CDL *see* Coal Distributors Limited

Cement Ltd, 108

Cement section, 105

Census, 1911, 53

Chipperfield, Miss, 64

Churchill, Winston, 82

City Quay, 21, 22, 26

Civil War, 78, 81

Clerys, 34

coal, 9, 10–12, 14–15, 73–4, 114
  decline in demand, 110–12
  decontrol, 1920, 75–6
  domestic consumption, 11–12,
    52
  General Strike, 82–3
  import licences, 96–7
  Irish, 20–1, 73–4
  merchants amalgamate, 103–4,
    120–2
  oil crisis, 1973, 130–2
  price control, 75–6
  prices, 6–7, 8, 23–4, 40, 66, 83–
    4, 121
  rationing 95, 96
  shortages, 73, 76, 87–8, 90
    Emergency, 93–7
    post-Emergency, 101–2
    theft of, 21

coal–cattle pacts, 76, 88, 89

Coal Controller, 66

Coal Department, 1–2, 2–3, 6–8
  accounts, 40
  import statistics, 10, 14, 16, 23,
    35, 51, 65, 89, 104
  post–Emergency, 101–2
  stock in trade, 27–8

Coal Distributors Ltd (CDL), 104, 106,
  123, 130–1, 133
  established, 121–2

Coal Emergency, 83

coal factors, 7–8

Coal Masters Association, 46

Coal Merchants' Association, 50, 59,
  60–1, 65, 66, 75, 82, 88, 120

Coal Emergency, 83
  Emergency, 97

Commercial Insurance Company, 88

computerisation, 132, 135

Conciliation and Arbitration Boards, 56

Connolly, James, 54–5, 56, 61, 62

Control of Manufactures Acts 1932–4,
  100, 108

Cork, 16, 45, 52, 93, 96, 112, 119,
  139, 141, 143

'corner-boys', 7–8

Cosgrave, William, 81

Coster Brodie, 25

Cox, Arthur, 79

Craig, Charles, 130, 144, 147

Craig Gardner, 35, 119

Crowley, Michael, 36

Cullen, Louis, 28

Cumann na nGaedheal, 79

Custom House Dock, 30, 34–5, 41,
  42–3, 51, 60, 65, 78, 82
  rental dispute, 74
  weighbridge, 63

customs duties, 19–20

Dáil Eireann, 16, 50, 68, 88
  Hewat in, 78–81

Daly, P. T., 79

de Valera, Eamon, 68, 81, 86–7, 89–
  90, 91, 109

debtors, 25

Dickinson, Page, 33

Dillon, David G., 147

Do–It–Yourself (DIY), 106, 138–9, 144

dockers, 44–6, 53, 81–2, 94–5

Dockrells, 117, 126

Dodder river, 10

Dohertys, 101, 120, 121

Dollard and Co., 25

Donnellys, 121

Dowling, Miss, 33

Drogheda, Marquess of, 25

Dublin, 5–6, 33, 52, 141, 143

bombs, 119–20
coal imports, 14
import duties, 20
import statistics, 16
lockout, 1913, 32, 59–62
population shift, 115
Dublin Bay Sailing Club, 19
Dublin Businessmen's Association, 50, 78, 81
Dublin Chamber of Commerce, 28, 50, 54, 78, 88
Dublin Commissioners, 83
Dublin Corporation, 34, 55, 64
Dublin Horse Show, 33, 59, 114
Dublin Port and Docks Board, 20, 28, 36, 50, 74, 80, 88, 96, 121
Dublin Stock Exchange, 31, 110, 117
Dublin United Tramway Company, 31, 34, 50, 58, 66, 74–5, 83, 88
'duff', 97
Dún Laoghaire, 35, 43, 47, 50, 64, 74, 75
Dunlop, 77–8

Eason, Charles, 29, 60
Easons, 34, 58
East India Company, 22
Easter Rising, 1916, 65
economic policy, 108–10, 126–7
Economic War, 73, 76, 85, 87–8, 89
Eglantine, 29, 150
Electricity Supply Board (ESB), 96, 110
Emergency, 90, 91–100
emigration, 109
Employers Federation, 50
Engels, Frederick, 5
Engineering Department, 100, 107
Ennis, J. J., 72
Essex, Earl of, 6
Evening Press, 121

Ferguson Peacocke Ltd, 113
Fermoy mill, 133–4

Fianna Fáil, 81, 86–7, 89, 109
Findlaters, 34
First World War, 41, 47, 64–6, 68, 70, 88, 89, 93
FitzGerald, Garret, 110
Fitzwilton Group, 126
Forestry, Department of, 133–4
Freeman's Journal, 59, 60, 61–2
fuel oil, 104, 110

Gaelic Athletic Association (GAA), 141
Gaelic League, 54
Galway, 16, 141
General Motors, 78
General Strike, 1926, 2, 82, 86
Geoghegan, Jeannie, 116
George's Quay, 21–2, 26, 35, 65, 115, 118–19
new head office, 72–3
sale of, 129–30, 132–3
Glasgow, 30, 36, 40–1, 46, 85
Glen Abbey, 108
Gloucester Steelstock, 139
Good, John, 78
Goodbody Stockbrokers, 141–2
Goulding, W. & H. M., 108
Grand Canal, 51, 74, 75
Great Famine, 4, 5
Great Southern Railway, 93, 96, 97
Great Western Railway, 25
Gregory, Lady, 78
Guilford, James, 118, 147
Guilford, Ronald, 137, 147
Guilford, Sidney, 118
Guinness, 1, 34, 62, 74, 76, 83, 96
Guinness, John H., 147
Guinness and Mahon, 119

Hammond Lane Foundry, 104
Handipac, 111–12, 113
Hanlon, Thomas, 45
Hanna, James, 116, 124, 125, 130, 132, 134, 146, 148

Harper, Hugh, 64, 85, 146
Harper, Robert, 30, 36, 40–1, 146
 salary, 47
Havgast, 102
Healy, Maurice, 32
Heitoids, 99
Heiton, Isabella, 3–4
Heiton, James, 3–4
Heiton, Jane, 25
Heiton, Thomas, 3, 4, 5, 7, 13, 24–5,
 34, 133, 142
 sets up premises, 21
 shipping, 17
Heiton Holdings, 118
 diversification, 141–2
 investment in, 137–8
 management style, 137–8
 rationalisation, 132
 resurgence, 135
Heiton McFerran, 118–19, 125–6
Heiton Timber, 125–6
Heitons, 21–6, 53, 54, 108
 auction, 25–7
 capital base, 116–17
 decline in coal demand, 104–5,
  106, 110–12
 diversification, 106–7, 112–13
 under Hewat and Inglis, 28–31
 industrial relations, 58, 60–1, 81–2
 limited company, 31, 34–49
 merger declined, 69
 merger with McFerrans, 118–19
 shift from coal, 121–2, 124–7
 stock in trade, 1878, 27–8
 strategic planning, 106–7, 113,
  114–17
 technological developments, 74–5
Hellas, 22
Hely, Cecil, 116
Hely Group, 108
Herald, 34
Hewat, Anice D., 152
Hewat, Cecil, 82, 88, 93, 106, 117,

 146, 148, 152
 Iron Department, 114
Hewat, Elspeth, 80, 152
Hewat, J. Richard B., 147, 148, 152
Hewat, James, 80, 106, 114, 117, 124,
 146, 148, 152
 CDL, 121
 diversification, 113
 Handipac, 111–12
 oil crisis, 122–3
Hewat, Patrick D., 152
Hewat, Richard, 115, 126
 larger premises, 129–30
 Managing Director, 124
 new investment sought, 137–8
 objectives of, 139, 141
 sells George's Quay, 132–3
 sells Tara Street, 135
 timber outlet, 134
Hewat, Thomas, 21, 152
Hewat, William, 152
Hewat, William E. D., 68, 70, 93, 146,
 152
Hewat, William I, 27, 116, 146, 148,
 152
 death of, 38–9
 incorporation, 36
 partner with Inglis, 28–31
Hewat, William II, 38–9, 46, 48–9, 66,
 86, 146, 148, 153
 activities of, 50
 coal transport, 75
 death, 88
 industrial relations, 56, 60, 62
 political career, 78–81
 post-war report, 70, 72–3
 retires, 82
 salary, 46
 shareholding, 116–17
 staff committee, 63
 war bonuses, 68
History of a Black Diamond, The, 42,
 44, 94

Hollington, 138, 144
Home Grown Timbers Ltd, 133–4
Home Rule, 55
Homecare/DIY division, 144
horses, 47–8
Hospital Sweepstakes, 87
housing, 11, 115, 135, 142
Howth, Co. Dublin, 50
Hussey, James J., 146

Industrial Development Authority
    (IDA), 115, 133–4, 141
industrial relations, 44–6, 53–9, 64–5,
    73, 81–2
industrialisation, 14–15
Inglis, Sir J. Malcolm, 27, 48, 116, 146,
    148
    death of, 38–9
    incorporation, 36
    partner with Hewat, 28–9
Inglis, Robert, 28, 36, 48, 66, 146, 148
    salary, 47
Inglis, Vivian D., 47, 146, 148
Investment Bank of Ireland, 119
Investors in Industry, 137
Irish Citizens' Army, 62
Irish Coal Committee, 73–4
Irish Coal Importers Ltd, 120–1
Irish Exhibition, 1853, 15–16
Irish Independent, 34, 58, 118
Irish Life, 133, 137
Irish Oil and Cake, 96
Irish Press Group, 135
Irish Republican Army (IRA), 81
Irish Republican Brotherhood (IRB), 54
Irish Times, 108
Irish Transport and General Workers
    Union, 55–9, 81–2, 83
    Dublin lockout, 59–62
Irish Worker, 53, 57–9
Iron Department, 2–3, 13, 14, 36, 47,
    100, 110, 114, 119
    accounts, 40

    Emergency, 93–4
    increasing importance, 104–7
    rent, 76
    stock in trade, 27–8
    Iron Workshop, 105

Jacobs, 1, 34, 113
Jamesons, 1, 34, 96
Japan, 126
Jefferson Smurfit, 108
Johnson, Thomas, 80

Kane, Robert, 10
Kane, Sidney, 86, 102, 106, 120, 148
Kettle, Tom, 61
King, Frank, 141
Kingstown, 35, 43, 47, 74
Korean War, 99, 102, 103

Labour Party, 80, 87
Land Annuities, 87
Larkin, Jim, 55–9, 79, 81
    Dublin lockout, 59–62
Leeson, Mr, 47, 64, 68
Lemass, Seán, 106, 109
Liffey river, 10
Limerick, 16, 119, 122, 141, 143
    soviet, 68
Longford, Earl of, 25
Lord Mayor, 8, 9
Lowther family, 7
Lyons, F. S. L., 91

Macalister, J. Denham, 3, 47, 82, 86,
    146, 148
McArthurs, 27
McCormick, John, & Co., 23
McCowens, 141
McDowel, John & Co., 25
MacEntee, Sean, 87
McFerran & Guilford, 117
McFerran, John, 118
McFerran, Keith, 118, 147

McFerran, Robert, 118
McGuinness, L., 95
McMahon, Brendan, 125–6
McMahon, Denis, 125, 147
Macnie, George, 36, 39, 146, 148
McQuaid, John Charles, Archbishop of Dublin, 120
McSherry, Louis J., 132, 147
Madden, Thomas, 27
Magennis, Professor, 79
Marshall Plan, 100
Martin, Leo, 138, 142, 147, 148
Martin, T. & C., 22, 25, 108, 117
Maxwell, Mr, 64, 68
Minch Norton, 96
Monaghan bombs, 119–20
Monsarrat, Nicholas, 92–3
Montpelier Products, 112–13
Morgan, Captain, 24
Morgan McMahon, 119
Mulcahy, General Richard, 78
Murphy, Thomas V., 147
Murphy, William Martin, 31, 34, 54, 56, 57, 58, 88
    Dublin lockout, 59–62
Murray, Mr, 45
Myles, John, 119

Naas Road, 119, 120, 129–30, 141
Napoleonic wars, 4
National Prices Commission, 121, 127, 129
National Union of Dock Labourers, 46, 55, 56
National Wages Agreements, 132
Nesbitt, Alexander, 48
Newbridge, Co. Kildare, 50, 74, 77
North Ash, 17, 18, 19, 25, 26, 29, 150
Northern Ireland (NI), 119

O'Callaghan, Mary, 148
Ocean Pier, 95
O'Connor, Stephen, 144, 147, 148

O'Doherty, Vincent, 147
office staff, 46–7
O Giollagain, James J., 47, 64, 68
O'Hara, Henry, 14
O'Higgins, Kevin, 81
oil crisis, 1973, 122, 125
O'Kelly, Seán T., 78
O'Malley, Ernie, 78
OPEC, 122, 125
O'Rahilly, Colm, 147
O'Reilly, Tony, 108, 112, 126

Peel, Mrs, 12
pensions, 86
Petty, Sir William, 6
Pim, Frederick W., 36, 146
Pims, 25, 34
Plumer, Mr, 47
Poland, 102, 103, 120
Poolbeg Street, 21, 26, 40, 118, 120
Presbyterian Association, 36, 38
Presentation Convents, 25
Provincial Bank, 27
public coal yards, 6

Quigly, Jane Francis, 4
Quirke, Diarmuid, 134, 147, 148

Ranks (Ireland), 108
Rathmines, 66
Ratified Chocolate Co., 58
Reid, Mr, 33
Ringsend, 51, 74, 77, 82, 118
    new terminal, 121–2
Roache, W., 65
Roadstone Ltd, 108
Roe, George, distillers, 25
Rogerson, William Kennedy, 116
Royal Bank, 29
Russell, George, 61
Russia, 81, 101, 103
Ryan, John, 91

St Andrews College, 38
St Eunan, 96, 99, 151
   sold, 104
St Fintan, 82, 85, 151
   second, 100
   sold, 104
   sunk, 93, 95, 99
St Kenneth, 82, 85, 99, 100, 151
   sold, 104
St Kevin, 29, 41, 66, 150
St Kilda, 30, 35, 41
St Margaret, 35, 41, 66, 150
   sunk, 30, 70, 72
St Mirren, 35, 42, 66, 68, 70, 150
   repairs, 84–5
   sunk, 41
St Mungo, 82, 85, 89, 99, 151
   sold, 104
   sunk, 41, 66, 93
St Olaf, 35, 41, 42
St Patrick, 41, 66, 150
   sales depots, 8–9, 33, 43, 50, 74, 93, 143
'Scotch carts', 13
Scott, Sir Walter, 5
Searight, Miss, 64
Second World War, 89–90, 91–100
Select Committee on Combinations of Workmen, 45
Senator Possehl, 102
Shannon hydroelectric scheme, 3, 80
shipbuilding, 45–6
Shipping Department, 3, 16–20, 22–5, 36
   accounts, 40–1
   crews, 102–3
   damage, 41
   duties, 19–20
   Emergency, 93–7, 99–100
   fleet, 149–51
   investment in, 29–30
   losses, 84–5
   ships sold, 104

size of cargo, 41–4, 102
   unloading, 22, 34–5, 42–3, 94–5
Sick and Indigent Room Keepers' Society, 11
Simmons, Martin, 138
Simmons, Martin E., 147
Sinn Féin, 68
Sligo, 16, 141
Smith, Elizabeth, 15
Smiths' Potato Crisps, 107, 113
Smurfit, Michael, 108
socialism, 54–5
Somerville and Ross, 52
Souvenir Booklet, 1946, 105
Spencer Dock, 47, 51, 65, 74–5, 78, 82, 97
SS Flandria, 41
SS Mourne, 41
stables, 47–8, 76
staff, 86, 138
Staff Committee, 63–4, 76, 111
Standard Chartered Bank, 137
Standard Life, 137
Stanley, John, 23
steam cranes, 22, 30, 35, 72
steam engines, 14–15
Steel Department, 130, 139, 141, 143–4
Stephen Stokes Ltd, 122
Stokes Brothers and Pim, 115
strikes, 35, 46, 55–6, 64–5, 73, 81–2, 82–3
   lockout, 1913, 59–62
   miners, 76
Suez Crisis, 102
Sun Life Insurance Co., 86
Sunbeam Wolsey, 108
Supplies, Department of, 90, 96, 97, 101
Suttons, 112
Swastika Laundry, 96, 97
Swift, Dean Jonathan, 7
Switzers, 31, 118, 138

Syren, 17, 149

Tara Street, 118, 119, 135
taxation, 9
Teare, Andrew H., 147
Tedcastle, Robert, 23
Tedcastle McCormick, 53, 59, 63, 69, 120, 121
Thom, Alex, printers, 25, 31
timber, 133–4
Todd, Burns, 21, 25
Todd, William, 4
Townsend Street, 35
transport, 13, 47–8, 62–3, 72, 75, 114
see also shipping
    notional charges, 76–7
Travemunde, 101
Treaty Ports, 92–3
turf, 10–11, 20–1, 83, 97–8, 102

Unidare, 108
United States, 2, 4, 55, 83, 88, 100, 101, 102, 122
Usher, Edward, 106, 114, 146

wages and salaries, 29, 30, 33, 44, 46–7, 68, 132
Wallace, W. E. G., 85, 96
War of Independence, 68
Waterford, 96, 130, 143
Welters society, 45
Westmoreland Street, 35, 72–3, 76
Whitaker, T. K., 106, 109–10
Whitehaven colliery, 6–7, 16
Whiteside, Hamilton, 47, 64, 82, 146
Winter, Adam, 27
Workers' Union of Ireland, 81–2

Yeats, W. B., 78
Yom Kippur War, 122, 125, 126